N. Mezey

ON THE ROAD TO
Same-Sex Marriage

Bob Cabaj dedicates this book to
all the friends who are no longer with us:
Tim Beckett, Paul Douglas, Jonas Fields,
Charlie Hannigan, Roger Horwitz, Robert Johnson,
Paul Monette, Eric Lameroux, Karl Laubenstein,
Ed Roginski, Tom Stehling, and David Walters.

He also dedicates this book to those
who are still here—some in and some not in relationships:
Mary Anne Badaracco, Chris Carmichael, Tony Dark,
Joel Frost, Graeme Hanson, Tom Magaraci,
Roger Mazur, Steve McDaniel, Roy Palmeri,
David Purcell, and Terry Stein.

David Purcell dedicates this book to his life partner,
Steve McDaniel.

ON THE ROAD TO
Same-Sex Marriage

A Supportive Guide to Psychological, Political, and Legal Issues

Robert P. Cabaj   David W. Purcell
Editors

Josey-Bass Publishers
San Francisco

This book was coauthored by David W. Purcell in his private capacity. No official support or endorsement by the Centers for Disease Control and Prevention is intended or should be inferred.

Substantial discounts on bulk quantities of Jossey-Bass books are available to corporations, professional associations, and other organizations. For details and discount information, contact the special sales department at Jossey-Bass Inc., Publishers (415) 433-1740; Fax (800) 605-2665.

For sales outside the United States, please contact your local Simon & Schuster International Office.

Jossey-Bass Web address: http://www.josseybass.com

 Manufactured in the United States of America on Lyons Falls Turin Book. This paper is acid-free and 100 percent totally chlorine-free.

Library of Congress Cataloging-in-Publication Data

On the road to same-sex marriage: a supportive guide to
  psychological, political, and legal issues/Cabaj, Purcell.
      p.   cm.
  Includes bibliographical references and index.
  ISBN 0-7879-0962-9 (alk. paper)
    1. Gay couples—United States. 2. Gay marriage—United States.
I. Cabaj, Robert P., date.   II. Purcell, David W., date.
HQ76.3.U50523   1997
306.84'8—dc21   97-24507
                                                                                  CIP

HB Printing   10 9 8 7 6 5 4 3 2 1   FIRST EDITION

Contents

Acknowledgments

We would both like to thank Steve McDaniel most of all for putting up with us as we crazily tried to meet our deadline and who helped balance our obsessiveness with calm acceptance and a great meal schedule. We will all remember the long Easter weekend of work in Atlanta when we persevered with the book and ignored the beautiful spring weather outside.

We also thank all the contributing authors for their hard work and attempts to keep to our tight schedule of deadlines and for working with us to improve the quality of the manuscript.

Bob Cabaj also wishes to thank his friends who watched him disappear, again, on many weekends to try and create this book while also juggling many other things. These friends include Mary Anne Badaracco; Chris Carmichael and Terry Stein; Tony Dark; Joel Frost and Tom Magaraci; Gerard Garcia and Don Tusel; Jim Guidera and Ed Parran; Graeme Hanson and Christopher Montgomery; Jeffrey Harding; Kew Lee; Roger Mazur; Chuck Meltzer; Roy Palmeri; and Demetri Politis. He also thanks his boss, Beverly Abbott, for her understanding about his crazy travels and overcommitment.

David Purcell would like to thank his supportive chosen family, including his partner, Steve McDaniel, as well as Susan Adams, Jim Burke, Leigh Hand (now deceased), Cindy Lancelot, Cathy McCall and Barbara Pennington, and Denise Mumley. They have all helped immensely over the past decade, and they share part of the responsibility for the wonderful place in his life he now finds himself. He also would like to thank his other friends and family, especially Cheryl Glickauf-Hughes, who have supported him in his personal growth.

Finally, we, Bob and David, each would like to thank the other for the mutual support given throughout the process of writing and editing this book. The final product is a result of an interaction of our diverse strengths. We started and ended this project as friends, a testament to our ability to rise above difficulties and disagreements that are an inherent part of the creative process of producing a book.

R.P.C.

D.W.P.

Introduction

ROBERT P. CABAJ AND DAVID W. PURCELL

Few recent topics have claimed as much media and political attention as the fight for the right of same-sex couples to marry legally. Striking at the heart of beliefs about sexuality, homosexuality, marriage, civil and legal rights for gay men and lesbians, the origins of sexual orientation, religious tenants about sex and marriage, child bearing and child rearing, adoption, divorce, custody rights, domestic partnerships, insurance benefits, and inheritance rights, the debate about same-sex marriage has caused a national and international furor.

Most people—especially Americans, who are raised in a society with ambivalent views about sexuality—are fascinated by sex. Homosexuality has been part of this fascination, approached with a mixture of both excitement and abhorrence. Things forbidden, of course, fascinate us, but homophobia and heterosexism, as defined later, also may make homosexuality appear repulsive.

The topic of marriage is almost as fascinating as sex. Marriage has clearly meant different things to different people in different cultures over time. Marriage has served as a core part of society: it has been a means of protecting and passing on property, of guaranteeing population growth, of symbolizing and solidifying a loving commitment. In addition, child rearing is often associated with marriage and, for many, may be the main purpose of a marriage. It is not surprising then that civil, legal, and religious tenants have developed over the centuries to codify and protect marriage and child bearing.

For the subject of same-sex marriage, the impacts of homophobia and heterosexism are important psychological factors that help to explain society's struggle with the topic. *Homophobia* can be defined as the fear or hatred of homosexuality itself; of people who are gay, lesbian, or bisexual; and of homosexual expressions of affection or sexual behavior. Homophobia may be expressed by merely ignoring or avoiding gay and lesbian people or any references to homosexuality; it may also include outright violence aimed at gay people or legal and religious sanctions against gay men and lesbians and against homosexual behavior. As we describe in *On the Road to Same-Sex Marriage*, most gay people themselves suffer from internalized homophobia, generated from being raised in a homophobic society, and must overcome this damaging psychological force in order to function well in the world.

Heterosexism, parallel to such concepts as sexism or racism, sees heterosexuality as the only acceptable form of sexual orientation and sexual expression. Because most people in the world are heterosexual, most see the world in a heterosexist way. At best, many heterosexuals do not even think about homosexuality or about gay and lesbian people; at worst, homophobic people wage outright attacks on gays and lesbians and seek to eliminate homosexuality. Again, homosexuality is not just seen as different but as somehow bad or sinful and thus deserving of ridicule or attack.

HISTORICAL PRECEDENTS AND LEGAL REALITIES

There are historical precedents for such attacks on gay men and lesbians. During economically poor times in European history, a diminished tolerance of homosexuality often led to discrimination or even persecution of those suspected of homosexual relationships. Veiled allusions to homosexuality can still be used to destroy careers in

Hollywood, in Washington, and elsewhere, as they were for years in England. Seeking out gay people became part of McCarthy-era blacklisting, and the decades-long, singularly relentless attack on gay men and lesbians in the U.S. military enjoys strong political, legal, and popular support to the present day.

The fight to remove sodomy laws and to establish legal and civil rights protections for gay men and lesbians has also affected the push for same-sex marriage. Many states still have sodomy laws that make certain sexual activities illegal and that, if enforced, are used almost exclusively against gay men and lesbians. It is hard to imagine winning the right to marry when sex between two men or two women is illegal in almost twenty states. In fact, the legal realities for gay men and lesbians can be shocking. For example, heterosexual privilege is so ingrained in our society that convicted heterosexual criminals, including murderers, maintain the right to marry in prison, regardless of the length of their sentence; yet gay men and lesbians in general struggle for basic acknowledgment of their relationships. AIDS and other life tragedies have shown gay men and lesbians how important it is to be legally connected. Being barred from hospital rooms and funerals, losing the right to participate in care, losing custody of a child, and being thrown out of a home after the death of a same-sex partner are all harsh realities known to lesbians and gay men.

The battle for nondiscrimination on the basis of sexual orientation is being fought on a city-by-city and state-by-state basis, with both victories and setbacks for gay people in places such as the states of Washington and Colorado and the cities of Cincinnati, Ohio, and San Francisco, California. Politicians have learned they can stir up voter interest by attacking gay men and lesbians and have learned to use such negative attitudes in their political campaigns. Only for a few, such as former congressional Representative Robert Dornan of Orange County, California, an extremely vocal homophobic politician who narrowly lost his congressional race, has this strategy backfired. Fortunately, popular support for gay men and lesbians is growing across the country, although a majority of Americans still oppose same-sex marriage.

It was not surprising to witness the political battle in the summer of 1996, just before a major presidential, senatorial, and congressional race, over the Defense of Marriage Act (DOMA). When a few gay and lesbian couples sued for the right to marry in Hawaii, based on an interpretation of a state statute on marriage, the rest of the United States suddenly sat up and took notice. People had to face the fact that gay men and lesbians might be able legally to marry their partners in Hawaii and then fly home to try to have their marriages acknowledged in other states. The press focused on the issue; some gay people began to hope; and the Christian right— a very strong political force in the United States—began to panic and started an unprecedented campaign against same-sex marriage.

It is important to recognize that not all gay men and lesbians welcome the possibility of same-sex marriage. First, some activists are angry that marriage has come to be a focal issue when in thirty-nine states people can still be fired from their jobs based on their sexual orientation. In reality, the gay community has not had much choice regarding timing, now that the Hawaii case is on the verge of being decided in a positive manner and is creating a frenzied backlash. Second, some gay men and lesbians think that marriage is a bankrupt heterosexual institution that should not be copied. However, a late 1996 poll in the *Advocate* found that 81 percent of gay men and lesbians would choose to marry if it were legal, while 10 percent would choose not to marry.

In 1996, the fight against same-sex marriage was linked to love of America and trust in its future, and most politicians jumped on the bandwagon to pass the DOMA. Even though the United States faced a similar issue in the 1960s when laws against mixed-race marriages (anti-miscegenation laws) were declared unconstitutional, Congress ignored the history and approved the DOMA just in time for the 1996 elections. In April 1996, a *New York Times* editorial predicted that same-sex marriages will be accepted in thirty years just as mixed-race marriages are today. The editorial noted that the backlash against such marriages was driven by "social intolerance" but that it also posed a threat to the nation's federal system of laws by setting up the possibility that marriages valid in one state would be invalid in another. (Chapter Six explores further the parallels between anti-miscegenation laws and anti–gay marriage laws.)

PURPOSE OF THE BOOK

On the Road to Same-Sex Marriage reviews the evolution and development of the current situation on gay and lesbian marriage, with a focus on psychological and legal issues. While one of the chapters (Chapter Eight) focuses on religious and spiritual issues regarding same-sex marriage, most of the focus is on civil marriage because of the benefits bestowed on it by local, state, and federal governments. The book also examines the political and legal issues involved in seeking same-sex marriage that continue to be of general concern across the country. Various chapters explore how and why gay people form relationships (Chapters One, Four, and Five), how gay relationships differ from "straight" relationships (Chapter Four), and what the impact—beneficial and harmful—may be with legally sanctioned same-sex marriage on a variety of emotional, psychological, legal, and child rearing issues (Chapters Three through Seven). In addition, Chapter Eight looks at the various religions' and religious institutions' attitudes towards gay men and lesbians, and Chapter Nine completes the road to same-sex marriage by examining international trends.

We would like to emphasize that we do not necessarily urge gay men and lesbians to marry if it becomes an option. We are trying to emphasize that marriage for same-sex couples should be an available option—just as for opposite-sex couples—and each couple can decide to exercise that option or not. In a similar manner, arguing for gay men and lesbians in the military does not mean that gays and lesbians should join the military, but the option should be available on the basis of equality and fairness.

We hope that the book will be informative, entertaining, and provocative. There are many battles ahead for gay and lesbian civil, legal, and human rights. It is our intention that *On the Road to Same-Sex Marriage* serve as another weapon and road map in that struggle.

ON THE ROAD TO
Same-Sex Marriage

1

History of Gay Acceptance and Relationships

ROBERT P. CABAJ

*To fully appreciate how long and arduous the road
to same-sex marriage has been, we must view it from
a historical perspective. As this chapter will make
clear, same-sex relationships have existed throughout
recorded history and have been sanctioned by laws
and even religious rituals at various times and in
various places. To understand the current resistance
to legalizing same-sex marriage in America, it is also
essential to review the history of homophobia and the
evolution of the concepts of sex and gender. This
chapter maps out the road already traveled on the
journey toward same-sex marriage.*

The fight for and the resistance to legal same-sex marriage
continues to rage across the United States. How did this battle form, and how is it progressing? This book describes the road
that the current movement has followed to try to obtain legally
sanctioned civil marriages between two people of the same sex. This
chapter sets the historical perspective: it reviews the history of
homosexuality, same-sex relationships, and even same-sex marriages
over time, and it examines one of the most powerful and overwhelming factors in the battle: homophobia.

1

A BRIEF HISTORY OF HOMOSEXUALITY, HOMOPHOBIA, SEX, AND GENDER

Love between people of the same sex has been recorded through-out all of history in most countries and cultures. Sexual activity between people of the same sex also has been described across time. The acknowledgment and acceptance of such homosexual sexual behavior as well as the affectional (or loving) behavior between people of the same sex has varied over time and place. Though not actually acknowledged as a separate entity or "condition" by the medical and psychiatric establishment until 1869, homosexuality is an integral part of civilization and culture and has been described and understood in many different ways. Similarly, men and women who are primarily attracted to others of the same sex have also been described and understood in various fashions.

ANCIENT TIMES

Marriage is described in the Old Testament as an arrangement for procreation or for property protection. Some argue that the ancient laws of Cannan and Egypt, described in the Bible, allowed for mar-riage between a man and a man and a woman and a woman.

    Much is known about what we now call homosexuality and gay and lesbian people since the times of ancient Greece. Both homo-sexual sexual behavior and loving relationships between men were a well-tolerated part of life in Greek society. (As is common throughout history, very little is ever mentioned about relationships between women.) In fact, in parts of Greece, male relationships were officially sanctioned with state ceremonies. John Boswell, a historian who has written about homosexuality and same-sex rela-tionships in premodern Europe, implies that the relationships were often between two men of similar age and background, akin to mod-ern gay male relationships; but in fact—as was the custom in sanctioned sexual relationships between men—the couples were usually composed of an older man and an adolescent, both free and equal citizens. The marriage typically lasted until the adolescent grew into manhood, when he would usually leave that relationship and wed again to either a woman or a man, depending on his desire.

In Greece, there was no equation of homosexuality and effeminacy. Greeks admired the masculinity of powerful gay men, and mythology reflected the respect and acceptance of loving relationships between men. Ganymede, a modern symbol of gay men and homosexuality in the arts, was the beautiful son of the King of Troy, taken by Jove to heaven as his beloved and cupbearer. Some of the origins, though, of modern homophobia can be seen in the myth of Hercules, who had many male lovers. When he was punished for killing Ophitus in a fit of madness, he was forced to dress like a woman and do female chores for Queen Omphale, while she wore his lions' skins. In Greece, a male was punished by being made to act "effeminately," that is, made to act like a woman.

Rome and the Catholic Church

Our current concept of marriage and the ritual acknowledgment of it—something other than a man buying a woman or carrying a woman off in war to be with him and run his household—began to form in the first century C.E., through an interaction between the early Catholic Church and the various ruling states. In the first century, in ancient Rome, marriage between men was sanctioned, and the Emperor Nero is reported to have married a man in a very well-publicized public ceremony. Rome also had elaborate adoption laws and practices that allowed men to adopt each other and pass along property to one another.

By the fourth century, however, social tolerance and acceptance of homosexuality had weakened, partly due to the influence of the church and partly due to the economic downturn of the Roman Empire. (John Boswell describes the links between a poor economy and prejudice with the need to blame or scapegoat someone or some group of people.) A statute specifically outlawing same-sex marriages was passed, and the Roman pagan marriage ceremonies were changed to include the Catholic Church's rituals. Laws specifically aimed at prohibiting homosexual activity, and "men who chose to give their bodies to other men like women" were condemned to be burned at the stake.

In parts of Greece and parts of the Orthodox West and East, however, formal rituals and blessings of same-sex relationships remained in effect officially until the fourteenth century, though such marriages were recorded and acknowledged well into the twentieth century. The ninth-century Greek emperor, Basil, was married as an adolescent to a male, then married an adolescent when he became a man, and later married a woman.

Marriage as institution and as ritual were further codified and defined throughout the following centuries. Marriage of blood relatives were excluded, and adultery was defined in England; marriage was defined as a religious contract in Islamic countries, and marriage was made a sacrament in the Catholic Church in the twelfth century. The church was granted exclusive power to execute marriages in most of Europe.

Any marriages or blessings of same-sex relationships from the sixteenth century onward occurred typically in countries influenced by Greek laws and culture, though there appears to have been same-sex marriages performed by the Catholic Church in Rome in the 1570s (many of the couples were subsequently burned at the stake in public). Homosexuality itself and the men who had sex with other men were, again, tolerated or persecuted in various cycles throughout the Middle Ages, with the most severe condemnations beginning in the twelfth century and continuing until this century. In Scandinavian countries, however, men having sex with other men was acceptable, as long as a man was not the receptive or passive sexual partner too often; if he were not the active partner most of the time, he would be ridiculed.

Middle Ages and the Renaissance

The concepts of sex and gender also changed and evolved throughout the Middle Ages. Randolph Trumbach, a historian of homosexual behavior, describes how Western Europe conceptualized three, then four, genders: until the eighteenth century, gender roles, activities, and behaviors were conceptualized as (1) male (or masculine) and usually associated with men; (2) female (or feminine) and usually associated with women; and (3) "sodomites" or "mollies," usually associated with adult passive effeminate males who often dressed as women and who exclusively desired men sexually. In the early 1800s, the fourth gender construct of "sapphites" or "tommies" was recognized, usually associated with adult assertive women who often dressed as men and who preferred sexual activities with women.

In addition, three sexes were conceptualized—man, woman, and hermaphrodites. This conceptualization operates even today, although hermaphrodites (people with ambiguous genitalia) are rarely considered in discussions of sex. (In modern times, if ambiguous genitalia are discovered at birth or in early childhood, the child is usually assigned to one sex or the other and may also undergo surgery to create genitalia to match the assignment of male or female.)

Until the nineteenth century, hermaphrodites usually chose to be considered one sex or the other, and it was believed that all sexes could be sexually active with any sex. A fairly rigid hierarchy of sexual behavior was defined: older males could penetrate younger males or women, but women were not to penetrate men, or younger men penetrate older men. (*Penetrate* could be defined as the actual insertion of a penis or dildo or as more active, aggressive, or initiative sexual activity.) To violate the correct order was considered sodomy.

Until the fifteenth century, effeminacy in men was equated with the presence of emotional traits or actions considered appropriate to women, especially passive anal intercourse or "acting like a wife," with little bias or judgment of such behavior or traits. The Renaissance, however, ushered in the current era of resistance to ambiguity and of differences and polarization of the sexes and sex roles. For the first time, hermaphrodites were associated with androgyny and homosexuality. Bisexuality was acknowledged but associated with homosexuality. Males were seen as active by nature, women were seen as passive, and passivity in men was disapproved and ridiculed. Men were strong and performed actions, and women were weak and acted upon. As is clear, such thinking continues to this current day, though the feminist movement has helped encourage a rethinking of gender roles of both males and females.

THE ROOTS OF HOMOPHOBIA AND ANTI-GAY DISCRIMINATION

Homophobia can be seen as having its origins in these past times. *Homophobia* can be defined simply as the fear or hatred of homosexuality itself, of people who are gay or lesbian, or of same-sex expressions of affection or sexual behavior. Feminine gender behavior was seen as a weakness in men, and "effeminate" men were thought to be deficient in masculine power and to lack virile qualities such as bravery and aggression. Such men would presumably act passively with other men; that is, choose to act like a woman, and therefore be targets of the same pejorative generalizations aimed at women. In fact, men would be punished by being forced into sexual submission, as recounted in a sixteenth-century story titled "Tale of the Youth Who Was Caught in the Act of Adultery and Was Sodomized and Flogged by the Husband."

Such beliefs about effeminate men combine with the heterosexism of the dominant worldview to create a strong basis for homophobia. Since most people are heterosexual, they assume everyone is and either ignore or even attack other forms of sexual affection and behavior. Most heterosexuals cannot understand the attraction of men for each other or women for each other, and assume that the man who desires another man is in some way like a woman. Such a man will be seen as "effeminate," whether he is or not, and as deserving of ridicule and bias. The belief that gay men are similar to women, when combined with the heterosexism and sexism of the Western world, certainly can explain the origins of a socially condoned homophobia, one that is usually aimed at gay men more than lesbians.

The 1800s witnessed increased societal homophobia and unprecedented attacks on gay people, especially in England, with more laws outlawing sex between people of the same sex. In England, effeminacy was not only equated with homosexuality but also with the aristocracy and thus the popular notion of the "fop" and the dissolute, sexually wanton upper classes. Such thinking helped support the social agenda of the time, which was to foster and support the common man and the middle class; if the upper class was seen as weak, effeminate, and holding back the common man, so much the better to support social unrest and turmoil. Effeminate men were seen as open targets to attack and eliminate.

The link between stigma and prejudice are well studied in the psychiatric and sociological literature. The stigmatized group is seen as different and defective. The victims of stigmatization usually become withdrawn, passive, and helpless. When applied to gay men, such traits in the stigmatized group can be seen as effeminate and foster the thinking just described. Most stigmatized groups, even if seen as weak or passive, eventually become feared for their differences and therefore are seen to deserve discrimination. If the discrimination and stigma are very strong, the targeted group is seen as one that should be isolated and not allowed to mix with other groups or share in the comforts, rights, and privileges of the dominant society. Again, this summary of the stigmatization, prejudice, and discrimination process explains much of the present-day attitudes toward gay and lesbian people and the resistance to having them participate in the institutions, such as marriage, available in the larger society.

The Americas

When explorers arrived from Western Europe, they of course dis-covered many customs and practices very different from those with which they were familiar. Marriage had different customs and dif-ferent meaning among the various Native American peoples. A book about the West Indies from 1552 described men marrying other men, though one of the men was usually castrated or impo-tent and acted like a woman. In precolonial Brazil, some native women who gave up the culturally accepted tasks of a woman and acted like men were known to be considered married to other women. There has been a long tradition in many North American native tribes of men marrying men; one of the men usually takes on traditional female roles or may be the sacred and revered *bedarche*, also known as two-spirit leader, who combines traits and duties of both men and women. From colonial times to the present, many same-sex couples have existed but were usually married as if they were members of the opposite sex, with one of the partners usually living dressed or disguised as a member of the opposite sex.

Modern Times and Psychiatry

Marriage as an institution, which includes rules about who is allowed to marry whom, has continued to be defined and codified through the twentieth century and around the world. For example, in the United States, interracial marriages were banned in most states beginning in 1661, as is described elsewhere in this book. In some countries, slaves, cripples, epileptics, certified insane people, and blind people were not allowed to marry.

After the church began oversight of the institution of marriage in the twelfth and thirteenth centuries, civil marriage (that is, mar-riage controlled by the government) disappeared for hundreds of years. But by the early 1900s, most countries had both civil and reli-gious marriages. Some same-sex marriages were noted in the United States over the last two centuries, but they usually involved a couple in which one party was a cross-dresser and lived publicly as if he or she were a member of the opposite sex; thus the couple passed as a heterosexual couple.

At the same time that civil marriage was making a comeback, the purpose of marriage gradually shifted from property protection and family unification for financial or political gain, to public sanctions of individuals' love and devotion. Procreation was, however, a central tenet of marriage throughout most of history. Only modern times have allowed love expressed in marriage without the absolute expectation of producing children.

Psychiatry was born in the late 1800s, in a Victorian era steeped in the thinking and conceptualizations described earlier—in the strict definitions of gender roles and purposes of marriage. Psychiatry has until recently perpetuated the homophobia and heterosexism so well established in our Western cultures. Sigmund Freud, however, did not see homosexuality as a mental illness and believed people could not change their sexual orientation. He believed that all people are born bisexual and develop into heterosexuals or homosexuals. He did, however, imply that homosexuality was a developmental arrest, and many psychoanalysts and other mental health professionals subsequently took this as a jumping-off point to consider homosexuality as some type of psychopathology, personality or character problem, or even a mental illness.

Freud did believe in rigid gender roles and saw many gay men as passive. His colleague Otto Fenichel also believed in strong gender roles but did acknowledge that they may be culturally determined; he believed gay men choose to be passive and, thus, choose their homosexuality. Psychoanalyst Helena Deutsch believed lesbians had not learned how to sublimate their aggressive energy into the culturally acceptable passivity associated with women and thus became homosexual.

In the United States, psychoanalysis became the rage in the 1930s through the 1950s, and almost every human behavior or trait was subjected to psychoanalytic examination. Homosexuality was a favorite subject and was inevitably described as pathological. In World War II, a closeted gay psychiatrist, Harry Stack Sullivan, helped set up the screenings used to try to identify gay people and prevent them from joining the military—a screening process and prejudice that continues to this very day. He described how to look for signs of effeminacy in men and masculinity in women and even suggested that gay men might lack a gag reflex (presumably from so much oral sex?) and could be screened through a physical examination.

Irving Bieber and Charles Socarides promoted the notion that gay men were made gay by their family upbringing and thus could change their sexual orientation with psychoanalysis and intensive psychotherapy. They and their followers attempted to "cure" hundreds of gay people, usually using reports of heterosexual sexual activity or marriage to a person of the opposite sex as the measure of success. They failed to note that, invariably, the gay person's inner sexual desires and fantasies remained homosexually oriented, and sexual behavior usually returned to homosexual behavior shortly after therapy ended, resulting in many unhappy marriages and frightened, confused, depressed, and anxious gay people.

Socarides still promotes his ability to cure gay people and has testified against civil and legal rights for gay people from the 1960s to the present, as described elsewhere in this book. He and other colleagues support an intervention called reparative therapy, based on the notion that poor parental upbringing causes gay men to lack masculinity and lesbians to lack femininity. Their therapy is based on the belief that teaching gay men how to be more masculine or play sports and teaching lesbians how to be more feminine and put on makeup will change their sexual orientations. They believe a gay person is better off heterosexual and married to someone of the opposite sex, even if they have to pretend or to deny their own innate sexual orientation. Such homophobic and heterosexist thinking invariably confuses gender roles and gender activity with sexual orientation.

CHANGES IN KNOWLEDGE ABOUT AND ATTITUDES TOWARD GAY PEOPLE

Legal challenges and attempts to fight discrimination against gay men and lesbians first gained real momentum and attention in the late 1800s in Germany and the early 1900s in England and America. Homosexuality as a medical or psychiatric entity was first identified in 1869, and the first attempts to study it, other than as a psychopathological condition, did not occur until the late 1940s.

American Psychiatry

Reflecting the belief of psychoanalysts of the times, the American Psychiatric Association in 1952 included homosexuality as a mental illness in the *Diagnostic and Statistical Manual of Mental Disorders*, known as the *DSM*, the official list of mental illnesses. Since most gay people did not feel guilty or upset about being gay, as the psychoanalysts believed they should, homosexuals were to be considered psychopaths or sociopaths; that is, people who lacked conscience or moral fiber. This way of seeing gay people is still the official view of the Immigration and Naturalization Services of the United States.

In 1968, the revised *DSM* classified homosexuality as a nonpsychotic mental disorder, along with other sexual "deviations." Finally, after years of effort and scientific data, described in the following section, homosexuality as a mental illness was removed from the *DSM* in 1973. A compromise diagnosis, known as ego-dystonic homosexuality, was substituted, but, through the testimony and presentation of scientific data by myself and other gay and lesbian leaders in the mental health field, it was removed in 1986.

The New Thinking on Homosexuality: Kinsey and Hooker

The de-pathologizing of homosexuality was a long and difficult battle, and the attitudes of society at large and even many mental health professionals has not completely changed with the elimination of homosexuality from the *DSM*. For many people, homosexuality is a crime, a sin, or a sign of severe emotional disturbances. According to this view, homosexuals should not be allowed to express themselves and, most certainly, should not be allowed to marry each other.

Alfred Kinsey opened the possibility of new perspectives on homosexuality with his studies of the sexual behavior of men and women in the United States. He and his colleagues undertook a survey of the sexual practices of men and woman, with a review of all possible sexual combinations. He gauged sexual behavior on a scale from 0 for exclusive heterosexual behavior to 6 for exclusive homosexual behavior. His studies have been criticized for a variety of reasons, including poor sampling (mostly white college students and prisoners), but they certainly made Americans aware of sexuality and sexual behaviors previously rarely discussed. Kinsey's data are based strictly on reports of sexual contact resulting in orgasm. Using this definition, Kinsey found that 37 percent of the male population had some homosexual experience between the beginning of adolescence and old age. Of unmarried males who were thirty-five years of age or over, almost 50 percent had had a homosexual experience since the beginning of adolescence. Kinsey found that 4 percent of the white male population was exclusively homosexual throughout their lives. A study of the sexual behavior of women showed percentages of women having had homosexual encounters to be roughly one-half of the parallel categories for men. Most people fell in a bisexual range from 1 to 5; that is, not behaving exclusively heterosexually or homosexually. Again, Kinsey only studied sexual behavior, not sexual orientation.

The psychologist Evelyn Hooker can be credited with initiating changes in thinking about homosexuality within the mental health field. Undertaking research that met with great resistance and even ridicule, she demonstrated that there were no discernible differences between the psychological testing profiles of gay men and heterosexual men. Her findings effectively began the dismantling of the theory that gay men were psychopathological.

These changes, such as viewing homosexuality as a normal variation of human sexual and affectional expression, ushered in the notion that sexual orientation is a complex phenomenon with many variations along a spectrum of heterosexuality to homosexuality. They have opened up vast areas of knowledge about sexual orientation itself, the expression of sexual desire, the psychological and social forces that influence the lives of people with homosexual and bisexual sexual orientations, and the life cycles of such men and women.

The New Thinking on Homosexuality: Current Psychiatric Literature

The Kinsey Institute supported a variety of limited surveys and studies looking at both sexual behavior and sexual orientation, concluding that, with a path analysis of all the data known about homosexuality available to them at the time, homosexuality must, by default, be innate and not influenced developmentally by family upbringing. Other more recent studies on the biology, genetics, and familial patterns of sexual orientation add further support to that conclusion.

Other surveys noted that gay men and lesbians are a diverse and varied group and that there was no uniform way to be or become gay or lesbian in our society. The Kinsey Institute looked at how some gay and lesbian people were coupled—in open or closed relationships, between relationships, or not in relationships—to categorize the sample.

The psychoanalytic literature has begun to reflect these new perspectives. Psychoanalyst Richard Isay makes the assumption that sexual orientation is probably biologically based and looks at how some subtle or not-so-subtle aspects of the gay son may be recognized and responded to by the father, leading the father to withdraw from or treat that son differently than a heterosexual son. He thus looks at the triangle of the distant father/overinvolved mother/gay son, described by Irving Bieber, not as the cause of homosexuality but as a possible consequence of antecedent homosexuality or gender-non-conforming behavior.

Female homosexuality also has been studied and reviewed from the perspective that it is not pathological. The literature on gender and gender roles offers additional ways to look at both male and female homosexuality and is particularly useful in understanding the issues facing same-sex couples. For example, Carol Gilligan points out the divergent paths for male and female development: boys are brought up to be not like mother—to be different from an important nurturing figure—whereas girls are brought up to be like mother—closely identifying with the nurturing figure. Such an observation may help to explain the difficulty many male couples have with intimacy or the "fusion" or intense intimacy within many lesbian relationships, as described by clinicians working with same-sex couples.

Maggie Magee and Diana Miller have undertaken an extensive review of psychoanalytic thinking on female homosexuality, emphasizing the heterosexist and phallocentric assumptions. They conclude that there are no psychodynamic etiologies to female homosexuality and underline the need to see each lesbian (and, indeed, each person) as unique, without referring to stereotypic patterns.

The first major textbook on homosexuality that did not classify it as pathological was compiled and published in 1996 by myself and my coeditor, Terry Stein. Our book reviews all that is known about homosexuality and mental health and also reviews the efforts to seek a biological or genetic basis for homosexuality and sexual orientation itself. Though it is still not totally proven, the roles of familial inheritance patterns (through the work of Richard Pillard and colleagues), genes themselves (through the work of Dean Hamer and colleagues), and other biological factors (through the work of Simon LeVay and others) hold more promise in explaining origins of homosexuality than does any psychological or psychodynamic understanding.

The History of the Study of Same-Sex Couples

There is a growing literature on what constitutes gay or lesbian couples or extended families and on couples and family therapy with gay men, lesbians, and bisexuals. Studying gay couples requires an understanding of the impact of internalized homophobia, anti-gay bias, and the issues involved when two people of the same sex—and similar culturally determined gender role expectations—attempt to meet, bond, and establish relationships. Such studies have progressed with the changes in attitudes about homosexuality over the last few decades.

Contrary to the popular myth that gay people have difficulty forming and staying in relationships, some of the Kinsey Institute surveys of gay men and lesbians categorized gay people by their relationship status: in open or closed relationships, in a series of relationships, or not in relationships. More than 60 percent of gay men and lesbians in America are currently in relationships.

Dave McWhirter and Drew Mattison developed a stage model for gay male relationships (the stages may also apply, with some alterations, to lesbian couples and to heterosexual and bisexual relationships) and discussed how the stages may be useful in understanding clinical problems. The stages are

Stage I: Blending, marked by merging, romantic love, equalization, and high sexual intensity and activity

Stage II: Nesting, marked by homemaking and compatibility, along with ambivalence and decreased romantic love and sexual activity

Stage III: Maintaining, marked by re-emergence of the individual, risk-taking, and increased conflicts, along with establishment of traditions

Stage IV: Building, marked by collaborating, increasing productivity, and independence, with the ability to count on partner

Stage V: Releasing, marked by trusting, merging of finances and possessions, and taking the partner for granted

Stage VI: Renewing, marked by security, inward dwelling and remembering, and restoring the partnership

These stages and movement through them are quite fluid and somewhat tied to the longevity of the couple but are influenced as well by age, health factors, and social pressures.

Elsewhere I have proposed looking at four sets of variables to form a complete picture for understanding gay and lesbian couples. The individuals bring in their own progessions through the life cycle, maturity, possible mental health problems, and cultural factors. The individuals also have moved at their own rates in their gay or lesbian sexual orientation and identity development, including openness about sexual orientation, coming out to family and friends, and dealing with the effects of internalized homophobia. The relationship will be in one of the stages just noted, or might be expected to be in one, based on the length of the relationship; but discrepancies between the partners may exist. Finally, additional factors such as health, finances, children, and influences of families of origin will affect relationships.

In the context of understanding lesbian couples, the concept of merging is often discussed—the intense connection or even fusion of the two individuals in the relationship. Though this phenomenon is not unique to lesbian couples, such couples have been studied, and a specific psychotherapeutic technique known as "intimacy though distancing" was developed to help them.

Striving for Legal Same-Sex Marriage

As other chapters in this book make clear, the desire to marry is deeply ingrained, and the desire to have acknowledgment of and acceptance of a relationship is quite natural and powerful. It is not surprising that the attempt to legalize same-sex marriages parallels the emergence of gay liberation and the seeking of gay rights, which began in the 1950s in the United States and was clearly defined as a movement by 1969, following the Stonewall riots in New York City. The attempts to marry have continued despite legal sanctions, expense, emotional distress, public scrutiny, and even harassment and ridicule.

In 1970, a gay male couple attempted to obtain a legal marriage in Minnesota, only to be refused; the refusal was supported by the State Supreme Court. In 1973, the same thing happened for a lesbian couple in Kentucky. In 1974, a lesbian couple tried to marry in Ohio, and in 1975, several same-sex marriages were performed in Colorado, until halted by the state attorney general. Also in 1975, a marriage license was granted to a lesbian couple in Maryland, as was one to a gay male couple in 1982 in Colorado. In 1991, a male couple failed to be allowed to marry in Washington, D.C., and, of course, the attempt by two lesbian couples and a gay male couple to marry in 1990 in Hawaii led to the current efforts.

The recent history of religious institutions and same-sex marriage has been influenced by the following events. In 1984, the Unitarian Universalists Association recognized and affirmed that many of its ministers conducted same-sex unions, and in 1993, the General Assembly of the Union of American Hebrew Congregations supported legal sanction of same-sex unions. Chapter Eight reviews events that followed, as well as other religious institutions and their stances on same-sex marriage.

DEVELOPMENTAL ISSUES

While the world has grown, over time, in its awareness of and acceptance of gay men and lesbians, every gay and lesbian person today has to go through his or her own personal journey of awareness and acceptance. All gay and lesbian people have their histories in developing gay or lesbian identities. The issues that gay people need to deal with in growing up and forming a solid sexual identity have changed over time. A look at the current developmental issues for gay men and lesbians will demonstrate the harmful role of homophobia and the efforts gay people must make to overcome the effects of internalized homophobia so they can have a comfortable place in the world. Homophobia has played a part in the battle against same-sex marriage and it affects the level of comfort gay individuals experience in entering relationships.

There are three major tasks gay people have to undertake that heterosexual people do not. First, they need to recognize that there is indeed something about their sexual and affectionate feelings that is different from those of the majority. Second, they will need to *come out*; that is, to acknowledge first to themselves and then eventually to others that they have a different sexual orientation. Third, they will need to deal with internalized homophobia and possibly confront both heterosexism and anti-gay bias in coming out to others and living in the world as openly gay or lesbian. Each individual entering into a same-sex relationship will have negotiated these tasks to various degrees of success.

Being Different

The literature on the psychology of being different is very helpful in understanding some basic developmental issues. Learning to live in a society that does not readily accept difference shapes the sexual identity development of many children who will grow up to be gay, lesbian, or bisexual as they move from childhood into latency period. Carmine de Monteflores in particular describes how difficult it is growing up different. Whereas a person of color cannot hide skin color, and the difference is obvious to all, a person with a homosexual or bisexual orientation, while aware of being different, may not be recognized as different by anyone else. In a society that promotes and supports heterosexuality, the sense of difference in these children may be confusing and alienating, leading to social isolation and denial of natural feelings. For those children who are gender-discordant in behavior, especially boys who may be effeminate, profound deficits in self-esteem are likely to result from being shunned, humiliated, and derided by their peers.

The vast majority of parents are heterosexual and raise their children either assuming that they will be heterosexual or not thinking about their sexual orientation at all. For the child who will grow up to be gay or lesbian, exposure to such nonconfirming behavior and parental expectations enhances the feelings of being different. As a coping mechanism, such children commonly learn to disconnect and dissociate from their true selves, their sexual orientation, and their feelings and adapt to parental expectations by creating and presenting a *false self*—behaviors and attitudes that are not genuine reflections of the true self.

If the parents cannot respond to or give support for what is unfamiliar or uncomfortable for them, they will either ignore those attributes of the child that suggest difference or try to change them. This process of ignoring may be quite subtle, a process of neglect similar to that described by the Swiss psychoanalyst Alice Miller in her early works. Miller's description of parents who form and deform the emotional lives of their talented or different children has strong parallels with the development of many gay children. Parental reactions clearly shape and then validate the expression of the needs and longings of their children; parents more frequently reward what is familiar and acceptable to them and discourage behavior and needs they do not value or understand.

Children are unlikely to have clear and positive role models of gay adults available to them. For example, the sexual orientation and relationship status of gay and lesbian teachers are rarely revealed, and there is little positive media attention given to gay men and lesbians. In adolescence, children's sexual feelings emerge with greater urgency, but there is rarely any context or permission for their expression. Adolescents in particular often reject and isolate those who are different, encouraging conformity and further supporting denial and suppression of emerging homosexual feelings in the gay or lesbian adolescent.

When adolescents who have disconnected themselves from any awareness of their homosexual feelings begin to recognize the source of their sense of difference—their sexual and affectional attraction to people of the same sex—they will have a great variety of reactions. Some may work even harder to suppress these feelings by isolating themselves and avoiding situations that may stir up their longings. Others may devote extraordinary energy to academic or career success to cover up their underlying shame and sense of being defective. Still other such young people may become depressed, isolated, guarded, and lonely, expecting to be rejected and ignored if their true feelings are revealed. Often these young people become ashamed not only of their sexual feelings but also of their bodies, their social interactions, and other aspects of themselves.

Coming Out

The easiest way to conceptualize coming out is to view it as a series of steps that an individual negotiates in his or her own time and at his or her pace, with periodic steps forward and backward. The individual must first become aware that his or her own sexual orientation is different from that of the majority. The next step is to accept the awareness and to begin to integrate it into a self-concept and to grapple with the negative feelings that may be associated with homosexuality.

Next, the individual may choose to act on the feelings, although some gay people with strong gay feelings do not engage in sex with others of the same sex. Finally, gay people need to make a series of life decisions about whether to let others know and whom to let know, such as friends, family, work colleagues and peers, teachers, and medical providers.

Heterosexism and Homophobia

Internalized homophobia and anti-gay bias, combined with heterosexism, are the major negative forces that gay men, lesbians, and bisexuals must deal with in our society. All gay people have internalized homophobia, having been brought up in a heterosexist society that tends either to promote prejudicial myths about gay people or to ignore gay and bisexual people in general. Anti-gay bias is found at every level in our society: legal, medical, scientific, religious, political, social, educational, and judicial.

Part of the development for most gay men, lesbians, and bisexuals is to come out to their family members and to seek family acceptance. This process may be quite rewarding but also carries the danger of outright rejection. For many gay and lesbian adolescents, the attempt to get their family fully to accept them by coming out has led to physical and verbal abuse or to being thrown out of the home, leaving them no choice but to run away and live on the streets.

Coping in a Homophobic World

Many gay people will create their own family—that is, a close network of friends that serves the needs conventionally met by families of origin. Becoming part of a couple is also an important developmental step for many gay men, lesbians, and bisexuals. As described, even though there is no legal sanction of such relationships yet, the majority of gay people are in relationships, and many are as fully committed as heterosexual couples are. Having or adopting children is yet another developmental step many individual or coupled gay men and lesbians are undertaking, and there is an ever-growing literature on gay or lesbian parents and the children of lesbian or gay parents.

CONCLUSION

History teaches us that gay and lesbian people have always existed, have always formed relationships, and have faced varying degrees of acceptance or discrimination throughout recorded history. Marriage or some form of recognizing relationships of same-sex couples has also existed throughout recorded history.

The current resistance to gay marriage is rooted in homophobia, which has its origins in the Renaissance and still instills members of our society with fear and hatred of men and women who do not seem to follow the socially accepted masculine or feminine stereotypes. Combined with the heterosexism of the modern world, such homophobia creates problems for gay people in coming out, being recognized and accepted by family, and being protected by society. Same-sex marriage, clearly a way to both acknowledge and stabilize the gay community, goes against the current grain of sentiment in the United States, in spite of centuries of history of support for and acknowledgment of same-sex relationships.

Religious institutions and the political and economic forces operating in our society combine to enforce the resistance to allowing gay people to progress along the inevitable road to legally sanctioned same-sex marriage. All of society will benefit when all members of society are treated as equals, with equal respect and with equal access to rights, protections, and legal support and sanction. It is my hope that same-sex marriage will soon be legal and will bring us finally back to where we were almost two thousand years ago.

References

American Psychiatric Association. (1968). *Diagnostic and statistical manual of mental disorders (2nd Edition)*. Washington, DC: Author.

American Psychiatric Association. (1980). *Diagnostic and statistical manual of mental disorders (3rd Edition)*. Washington, DC: Author.

American Psychiatric Association. (1987). *Diagnostic and statistical manual of mental disorders (3rd Edition, Revised)*. Washington, DC: Author.

American Psychiatric Association. (1994). *Diagnostic and statistical manual of mental disorders (4th Edition)*. Washington, DC: Author.

Bailey, J. M., & Benishey D. (1993). Familial aggregation of female sexual orientation. *American Journal of Psychiatry, 150,* 272–277.

Bailey, J. M., & Pillard, R. C. (1991). A genetic study of male sexual orientation. *Archives of General Psychiatry, 48,* 1089–1096.

Bailey, J. M., Pillard, R. C., Neale, M. C., & Agyei, Y. (1993). Heritable factors influence sexual orientation in women. *Archives of General Psychiatry, 50,* 217–223.

Bayer, R. (1987). *Homosexuality and American psychiatry*. New York: Basic Books.

Bell, A. P., & Weinberg, M .S. (1978). *Homosexualities: A study of diversities among men and women*. New York: Simon & Schuster.

Bell, A. P., Weinberg, M. S., & Hammersmith, S. K. (1981). *Sexual preference: Its development in men and women*. Bloomington, IN: Indiana University Press.

Berube, A. (1990). *Coming out under fire: The history of gay men and women in World War Two*. New York: Free Press.

Berzon, B. (1988). *Permanent partners: Building gay and lesbian relationships that last*. New York: Dutton.

Bieber, I., Dain, H. J., Dince, P. R., Drellich, M .G., Grand, H. G., Gundlach, R. H., Kremer, M. W., Rifkin, A. H., Wilbur, C. B., & Bieber, T. B. (1962). *Homosexuality: A psychoanalytic study*. New York: Basic Books.

Boswell, J. (1980). *Christianity, social tolerance, and homosexuality: Gay people in Western Europe from the beginning of the Christian era to the fourteenth century*. Chicago: University of Chicago Press.

Boswell, J. (1994). *Same-sex unions in premodern Europe*. New York, Villard Books.

Burch, B. (1986). Psychotherapy and the dynamics of merger in lesbian couples. In T. S. Stein & C. C. Cohen (Eds.), *Contemporary perspectives on psychotherapy with lesbians and gay men* (pp. 57–72). New York: Plenum.

Burke, P. (1996). *Gender shock: Exploding the myths of male and female*. New York: Anchor Books.

Byne, W. (1994). The biological evidence challenged. *Scientific American, 270*, 50–55.

Byne, W. (1995). Science and belief: Psychobiological research on sexual orientation. *Journal of Homosexuality, 28*, 303–344.

Byne, W. (1996). Biology and homosexuality: Implications of neuroendocrinological and neuroanatomical studies. In R. P. Cabaj & T. S. Stein (Eds.), *Textbook of homosexuality and mental health* (pp. 129–146). Washington, DC: American Psychiatric Press.

Byne, W., & Parsons, B. (1993). Sexual orientation: The biological theories reappraised. *Archives of General Psychiatry, 50*, 228–239.

Cabaj, R. P. (1988). Gay and lesbian couples: Lessons on human intimacy. *Psychiatric Annals, 18(1)*, 21–25.

Cabaj, R. P., & Klinger, R. L. (1996). Psychotherapeutic interventions with lesbian and gay couples. In R. P. Cabaj & T. S. Stein (Eds.), *Textbook of homosexuality and mental health* (pp. 485–501). Washington, DC: American Psychiatric Press.

Cabaj, R. P., & Stein, T. S. (Eds.). (1996). *Textbook of homosexuality and mental health*. Washington, DC: American Psychiatric Press.

Cass, V. (1996). Sexual orientation identity formation: A Western phenomenon. In R. P. Cabaj & T. S. Stein (Eds.), *Textbook of homosexuality and mental health* (pp. 227–251). Washington, DC: American Psychiatric Press.

Chauncey, G. (1994). *Gay New York: Gender, urban culture, and the making of the gay male world 1890–1940*. New York: Basic Books.

Chodorow, N. J. (1978). *The reproduction of mothering: Psychoanalysis and the sociology of gender*. Berkeley: University of California Press.

Chodorow, N. J. (1992). Heterosexuality as a compromise formation: Reflections on the psychoanalytic theory of sexual development. *Psychoanalysis and Contemporary Thought, 15*(3), 267–304.

Coleman, E. (1982). Developmental stages in the coming out process. *Journal of Homosexuality, 7*, 31–43.

de Monteflores, C. (1986). Notes on the management of difference. In T. S. Stein & C. C. Cohen (Eds.), *Contemporary perspectives on psychotherapy with lesbians and gay men* (pp. 73–101). New York: Plenum.

Deutsch, H. ([1932] 1965). Homosexuality in women. *Neurosis and character types: Clinical psychoanalytic studies* (pp. 73–101). New York: International Universities Press.

Dollimore, J. (1991). *Sexual dissidence: Augustine to Freud to Foucault*. New York: Clarendon Press/Oxford University Press.

Drescher, J. (1996). Psychoanalytic subjectivity and male homosexuality. In R. P. Cabaj & T. S. Stein (Eds.), *Textbook of homosexuality and mental health* (pp. 173–189). Washington, DC: American Psychiatric Press.

Duberman, M. B., Vicinus, M., & Chauncey, G. (1989). *Hidden from history: Reclaiming the gay and lesbian past*. New York: New American Library.

Epstein, J., & Straub, K. (Eds.). (1991). *Body guard: The cultural politics of gender ambiguity*. New York: Routledge.

Eskridge, W. N. (1996). *The case for same-sex marriage: From sexual liberty to civilized commitment*. New York: Free Press.

Fenichel, O. (1945). *The psychoanalytic theory of neurosis*. New York: Norton.

Gilligan, C. (1982). *In a different voice*. Cambridge, MA: Harvard University Press.

Haldeman, D. C. (1991). Sexual orientation conversion therapy for gay men and lesbians: A scientific examination. In J. C. Gonsiorek & J. D. Weinrich (Eds.), *Homosexuality: Research implications for public policy* (pp. 149–160). Newbury Park, CA: Sage.

Haldeman, D. C. (1994). The practice and ethics of sexual orientation conversion therapy. *Journal of Consulting Clinical Psychology, 62*, 221–227.

Halperin, D. M. (1990). *One hundred years of homosexuality*. New York: Routledge.

Hamer, D. H., & Copeland, P. (1994). *The science of desire: The search for the gay gene and the biology of behavior.* New York: Simon & Schuster.

Hamer, D. H., Hu, S., & Magnuson, V. L. (1993). A linkage between DNA markers on the X chromosome and male sexual orientation. *Science, 261,* 321–327.

Hanley-Hackenbruck, P. (1988) "Coming-out" and psychotherapy. *Psychiatric Annals, 18*(1), 29–32.

Herdt, G. (Ed). (1996). *Third sex, third gender: Beyond sexual dimorphism in culture and history.* New York: Zone Books.

Herek, G. M. (1996). Heterosexism and homophobia. In R. P. Cabaj & T. S. Stein (Eds.), *Textbook of homosexuality and mental health* (pp. 65–82). Washington, DC: American Psychiatric Press.

Highwater, J. (1997). *The mythology of transgression: Homosexuality as metaphor.* New York: Oxford University Press.

Hooker, E. (1957). The adjustment of the male overt homosexual. *Journal of Projective Technique, 21*(1), 18–31.

Hooker, E. (1996). Epilogue. In R. P. Cabaj & T. S. Stein (Eds.), *Textbook of homosexuality and mental health* (pp. 917–919). Washington, DC: American Psychiatric Press.

Isay, R. A. (1989). *Being homosexual: Gay men and their development.* New York: Farrar, Straus & Giroux.

Isay, R. A. (1996). *Becoming gay: The journey to self-acceptance.* New York: Pantheon Books.

Katz, J. N. (1992). *Gay American history, revised edition.* New York: Meridian.

Kaufman, P., Harrison, E., & Hyde, M. (1984). Distancing for intimacy in lesbian relationships. *American Journal of Psychiatry, 141,* 530–533.

Kinsey, A. C., Pomeroy, W. B., & Martin, C. E. (1948). *Sexual behavior in the human male.* Philadelphia: Saunders.

Kinsey, A. C., Pomeroy, W. B., & Martin, C. E. (1954). *Sexual behavior in the human female.* Philadelphia: Saunders.

Kirkpatrick, M. (1996). Lesbians as parents. In R. P. Cabaj & T. S. Stein (Eds.), *Textbook of homosexuality and mental health* (pp. 353–370). Washington, DC: American Psychiatric Press.

Klinger, R. L., & Cabaj, R. P. (1993). Characteristics of gay and lesbian relationships. In J. M. Oldham, M. B. Riba, & A. Tasman (Eds.), *American Psychiatric Press review of psychiatry, volume 12* (pp. 101–125). Washington, DC; American Psychiatric Press.

Krafft-Ebing, R. ([1898] 1922). *Psychopathia sexualis.* Brooklyn, NY: Brooklyn Physicians and Surgeons Book Company.

Krajeski, J. (1996). Homosexuality and the mental health professions: A contemporary history. In R. P. Cabaj & T. S. Stein (Eds.), *Textbook of homosexuality and mental health* (pp. 17–31). Washington, DC: American Psychiatric Press.

Krestan, J., & Bepko, C. (1990). The problem of fusion in the lesbian relationship. *Family Process, 19,* 272–289.

Kurdek, L. A. (1987). Sex roles, self schema and psychological adjustment in coupled homosexual and heterosexual men and women. *Sex Roles, 17,* 549–621.

Kurdek, L. A. (1991). The dissolution of gay and lesbian couples. *Journal of Social and Personal Relationships, 8,* 265–278.

Kurdek, L. A. (1992). Relationship stability and relationship satisfaction in cohabitating gay and lesbian couples: A prospective longitudinal test of the contextual and interdependence models. *Journal of Social and Personal Relationships, 9,* 125–142.

Kurdek, L. A. (1995). Lesbian and gay relationships. In A. R. D'Augelli & C. J. Patterson (Eds.), *Lesbian, gay, and bisexual identities over the lifespan: Psychological perspectives* (pp. 243–261). New York: Oxford University Press.

Kurdek, L. A., & Schmitt, J. P. (1986). Relationship quality of partners in heterosexual married, heterosexual cohabitating, and gay and lesbian relationships. *Journal of Personality and Social Psychology, 51,* 711–720.

LeVay, S. (1996). *Queer science: The use and abuse of research into homosexuality.* Cambridge, MA: MIT Press.

LeVay, S., & Hamer, D. (1994). Evidence for a biological influence in male homosexuality. *Scientific American, 270,* 44–49.

Lewes, K. (1988). *The psychoanalytic theory of male homosexuality.* New York: Simon & Schuster.

Magee, M., & Miller, D. C. (1996). Psychoanalytic views of female homosexuality. In R. P. Cabaj & T. S. Stein (Eds.), *Textbook of homosexuality and mental health* (pp. 191–206). Washington, DC: American Psychiatric Press.

Martin, A. D. (1982). Learning to hide: The socialization of the gay adolescent. *Adolescent Psychiatry, 10,* 52–65.

McNeil, J. J. (1985). *The church and the homosexual.* New York: Next Year.

McWhirter, D. P. (1993). Biological theories of sexual orientation. In J. M. Oldham, M. B. Riba, & A. Tasman (Eds.), *American Psychiatric Press review of psychiatry, volume 12* (pp. 41–58). Washington, DC: American Psychiatric Press.

McWhirter, D. P., & Mattison, A. M. (1984). *The male couple: How relationships develop.* Englewood Cliffs, NJ: Prentice-Hall.

McWhirter, D. P., & Mattison, A. M. (1984). Psychotherapy for male couples: An application of the staging theory. In E. S. Hetrick & T. S. Stein (Eds.), *Innovations in psychotherapy with homosexuals* (pp. 115–131). Washington, DC: American Psychiatric Press.

McWhirter, D. P., & Mattison, A. M. (1996). Male couples. In R. P. Cabaj & T. S. Stein (Eds.), *Textbook of homosexuality and mental health* (pp. 319–337). Washington, DC: American Psychiatric Press.

Miller, A. (1981). *The drama of the gifted child.* New York: Basic Books.

Miller, N. (1995). *Out of the past: Gay and lesbian history from 1869 to the present.* New York: Vintage Books.

Nicolosi, J. (1991). *Reparative therapy of male homosexuality: A new clinical approach.* Northvale, NJ: Jason Aronson.

Patterson, C. J. (1995). Lesbian mothers, gay fathers, and their children. In A. R. D'Augelli & C. J. Patterson (Eds.), *Lesbian, gay, and bisexual identities over the lifespan* (pp. 262–290). New York: Oxford University Press.

Patterson, C. J., & Chan, R. W. (1996). Gay fathers and their children. In R. P. Cabaj & T. S. Stein (Eds.), *Textbook of homosexuality and mental health* (pp. 371–393). Washington, DC: American Psychiatric Press.

Peplau, L. A. (1991). Lesbian and gay relationships. In J. C. Gonsiorek & J. D. Weinrich (Eds.), *Homosexuality: Research implications for public policy* (pp. 177–196). Newbury Park, CA: Sage.

Peplau, L. A., & Cochran, S. (1990). A relationship perspective on homosexuality. In D. P. McWhirter, S. A. Sanders, & J. M. Reinisch (Eds.), *Homosexuality/heterosexuality: Concepts of sexual orientation* (pp. 321–349). New York: Oxford University Press.

Pillard, R. C. (1996). Homosexuality from a familial and genetic perspective. In R. P. Cabaj & T. S. Stein (Eds.), *Textbook of homosexuality and mental health* (pp. 115–128). Washington, DC: American Psychiatric Press.

Pillard, R. C., Poumadere, J., & Carretta, R. A. (1982). A family study of sexual orientation. *Archives of Sexual Behavior, 11,* 511–520.

Pillard, R. C., & Weinrich, J. D. (1986). Evidence of familial nature of male sexuality. *Archives of General Psychiatry, 43,* 808–812.

Plato. (1991). *On homosexuality: Lysis, Phaedrus, and Symposium* (B. Jowett, Trans.). Buffalo, NY: Prometheus Books.

Saslow, J. M. (1986). *Ganymede in the Renaissance: Homosexuality in art and society.* New Haven, CT: Yale University Press.

Socarides, C. W. (1968). *The overt homosexual.* New York: Grune and Stratton.

Socarides, C. W. (1978). *Homosexuality.* New York: Jason Aronson.

Socarides, C. W., & Volkan, V. (Eds.). (1991). *The homosexualities and the thera- peutic process.* Madison, CT: International Universities Press.

Spencer, C. (1995). *Homosexuality in history.* New York: Harcourt Brace & Company.

Stein, T. S. (1996). A critique of approaches to changing sexual orientation. In R. P. Cabaj & T. S. Stein (Eds.), *Textbook of homosexuality and mental health* (pp. 525–537). Washington, DC: American Psychiatric Press.

Stein, T. S. (1996). Lesbian, gay, and bisexual families: Issues in psychotherapy. In R. P. Cabaj & T. S. Stein (Eds.), *Textbook of homosexuality and mental health* (pp. 503–511). Washington, DC: American Psychiatric Press.

Szymanski, M. (1991, Fall). Battered husbands: domestic violence in gay rela- tionships. *Genre.*

Tafoya, T. N. (1996). Native two-spirit people. In R. P. Cabaj & T. S. Stein (Eds.), *Textbook of homosexuality and mental health* (pp. 603–617). Wash- ington, DC: American Psychiatric Press.

Trumbach, R. (1991). London's sapphites: From three sexes to four genders in the making of modern culture. In J. Epstein & K. Straub (Eds.), *Body guard: The cultural politics of gender ambiguity* (pp. 112–141). New York: Routledge.

Weinberg, G. (1983). *Society and the healthy homosexual.* New York: St. Martin's Press.

Weinberg, M. S., & Williams, C. J. (1975). *Male homosexuals: Their problems and adaptations.* New York: Penguin.

2

Current Trends in Same-Sex Marriage

DAVID W. PURCELL

The journey continues in this chapter as we look at our contemporary surroundings. In the 1980s and 1990s, gay men and lesbians have become more open and are more understood and accepted by society. The current effort to institute legal same-sex marriage began in full force in mid 1993, when the Hawaii Supreme Court suggested that the state's refusal to grant marriage licenses to three same-sex couples might be unconstitutional. That decision catalyzed many legal and political efforts both for and against same-sex marriage throughout the United States. The journey has been made somewhat easier by the increasing availability of domestic partner benefits for same-sex couples in both the public and private sectors, although the benefits pale in comparison to those accorded to legally married couples.

An examination of current trends regarding same-sex marriage must be placed in a context that recognizes the meteoric rise in visibility experienced by gay men and lesbians in the 1980s and 1990s. Fueled partly by the AIDS epidemic, this visibility has translated into an increase in societal acknowledgment of the dignity of gays and lesbians as people and as citizens. For example, in 1996 in *Evans* v. *Romer*, the United States Supreme Court struck down a Colorado ballot initiative passed by the voters of the state that invalidated gay civil rights protections in four Colorado cities and disallowed future municipal or state political bodies from protecting gay civil rights. This decision marked a dramatic shift from the court's 1986 decision in *Bowers* v. *Hardwick* upholding state sodomy laws (which outlaw various nonprocreative sexual practice in almost twenty states). In 1986, the court felt comfortable denying us basic privacy rights because of society's "moral discomfort with homosexuality." In contrast, in 1996 the court held, by a 6 to 3 majority, that governments cannot make laws based solely on animosity towards others. The court remarked that Colorado could not "deem a class of persons a stranger to its laws" and that the only purpose of the ballot initiative was to make gay men and lesbians "unequal to everyone else."

Clearly, *Evans* v. *Romer* represents a shift in tolerance and maybe even an acceptance of us by the highest court in the land. As discussed in Chapter Seven, legal opinions regarding certain classes of people (for example, African Americans, gay men, and lesbians) do change over time, and these changes are heavily influenced by changing social mores. Another recent development that supports this trend of acceptance took place in May and June 1997 when New Hampshire and Maine became the tenth and eleventh states to provide civil rights protections to gay men and lesbians. Now all six states in New England provide some sort of protection. Of course, this general trend of increased societal approval has been accompanied by backlash, but overall, from 1981 to 1997 there has been a great increase in openness about and acceptance of us. This trend of acceptance and backlash is poignantly mirrored in the current debate about same-sex marriage.

The issue of same-sex marriages has vaulted to the forefront of the lesbian and gay civil rights movement in the 1990s. The increasing and intense focus on same-sex marriage rights for lesbians and gay men is more accidental than planned. It stems directly from a case that began in Hawaii over six years ago that may eventually make same-sex marriages legal in that state. This case still has not been finally settled, and it represents an important current trend that bears watching and understanding. In response to the Hawaii case, two contradictory trends have swept the country in the past few years. First, a federal law and many similar state laws have been passed since 1994 banning same-sex marriage or defining *marriage* as a union between a man and a women. In contrast, over the past ten to fifteen years, domestic partnership benefits have been granted by a growing number of governmental entities and private businesses, although not without some litigation and protest. This chapter makes clear that the road to same-sex marriage is similar to other civil rights movements; it is filled with twists and turns, setbacks and victories, but the overall direction is toward greater acceptance.

THE MOVE TOWARD LEGAL
SAME-SEX MARRIAGE IN HAWAII

The most notable current trend in same-sex marriage dates from December 1990, when three same-sex couples—two lesbian couples and a gay male couple—applied to the Hawaii State Health Department for marriage licenses. This act began a six-year court battle in the case now titled *Baehr v. Miike* (which is still ongoing) and a flurry of anti-gay marriage legislative activity at the national and state level. It also unintentionally placed the issue of same-sex marriage at the forefront of the civil rights movement for lesbians and gay men.

For years, same-sex marriage was not a priority issue for mainstream gay and lesbian organizations, partially due to the overwhelming popular opposition to it compared with other issues such as employment discrimination protection. For example, a May 1996 *Newsweek* poll found that 58 percent of respondents thought that gay marriage should be illegal, compared with 33 percent who thought that it should be legal. In contrast, the same poll found that

84 percent of Americans supported equal employment rights for gay men and lesbians. National gay groups did not want to waste resources on what was likely a losing effort. Gay marriage cases, such as the one filed in the District of Columbia by two gay men in 1991 or the *Baehr* case in Hawaii, received little support or enthusiasm. This pessimistic attitude seemed justified, especially when the first trial court ruling in *Baehr* dismissed the case outright.

Background Events

In May 1993, the Hawaii Supreme Court issued a decision that set the stage for same-sex marriage to be vaulted into the mainstream consciousness and placed at the forefront of the lesbian and gay rights movement. The court sent the case back to the trial court with the strong suggestion that the ban on same-sex marriage might be unconstitutional, and it required the state to show a compelling state interest in denying gay men and lesbians the right to marry. After this decision, national gay and lesbian groups rallied behind the same-sex marriage issue, and anti-gay groups began a campaign against such marriages.

When the case came back to trial in the fall of 1996, the state argued that the potential damage to children raised in same-sex households constituted a compelling state interest in not allowing same-sex marriages. This claim is one of the common myths identified by Greg Herek that has been used to deny lesbians and gay men a variety of civil rights, including contact with their own children. In contrast, the plaintiffs presented expert testimony based on scientific evidence showing that (1) children raised in lesbian and gay households are as well adjusted as those raised in homes headed by heterosexual couples; (2) sexual orientation does not affect parental fitness; and (3) same-sex and different-sex relationships do not differ in any way that negatively affects parental fitness. The plaintiffs also argued that denying marriage to same-sex couples denies children both the emotional and financial resources that a second parent provides.

More Recent Rulings in Hawaii

On December 3, 1996, Circuit Court Judge Kevin Chang declared the state's ban on same-sex marriage to be an unconstitutional infringement of equal protection rights under state law, citing the testimony of expert witnesses such as psychologist Charlotte Patterson. After the ruling, opponents of same-sex marriage prepared a series of actions to try to stop the ruling from ever taking effect. First, the state has appealed the decision to the Hawaii Supreme Court, whose decision will be final. A ruling is expected in late 1997, and a verdict in favor of same-sex marriages is predicted by many authorities. If the Hawaii Supreme Court rules in favor of same-sex marriage, the only thing that could stop same-sex marriages in Hawaii is an amendment to the state constitution.

In 1996, before the *Baehr* ruling, the Hawaii House of Representatives passed a constitutional amendment limiting the right to marry to heterosexual couples, but the Hawaii State Senate rejected the amendment. In early 1997, in response to the Circuit Court decision, the Hawaii Senate and House of Representatives passed different bills, each with a constitutional amendment banning same-sex marriages but providing that if the amendment is passed (on voter approval), same-sex couples get many of the rights and responsibilities of married couples. In April 1997, the two legislative bodies in Hawaii reached a two-part compromise: (1) in November 1998 voters will get to vote on an amendment to the state constitution banning same-sex marriage; (2) a package of sixty benefits, including hospital visitation rights, will be extended to "reciprocal beneficiaries." The Hawaii Supreme Court heard the appeal of Judge Chang's ruling in June 1997, and a decision is expected this year. The time lag makes it possible that Hawaii could start issuing marriage licenses to same-sex couples by the end of 1997, if the Hawaii Supreme Court upholds Judge Chang's ruling. The voters and the legislature would then be in the difficult situation of having to vote to void existing marriages in 1998.

THE PROLIFERATION OF LAWS BANNING SAME-SEX MARRIAGES

While the intensive legislative activity in Hawaii is partly in response to *Baehr*, a flurry of legislative activity also has occurred around the country over the past two years.

The Defense of Marriage Act

The broadest rejection of same-sex marriages occurred when the Defense of Marriage Act (DOMA) was overwhelmingly passed by the U.S. House of Representatives (342 to 67 in July 1996) and the U.S. Senate (85 to 14 in September 1996). President Clinton's midnight signing of the bill added insult to injury for many gay and lesbian activists, who protested DOMA's passage around the nation. DOMA defines *marriage* as the union between a man and a woman and allows states to deny recognition of same-sex marriages. The bill does not ban same-sex marriages but denies recognition of them by precluding spousal benefits distributed by various government programs such as Social Security.

State Legislative Actions Against Same-Sex Marriage

While same-sex marriages are not yet legal anywhere in the United States, the possibility that marriages might become legal in Hawaii led to a flurry of anti-gay and lesbian legislation. In 1996 and early 1997, anti-gay marriage bills were proposed in almost forty state legislatures and passed in over twenty states. In 1997 alone, five state anti-gay marriage laws have passed, while seven have failed. Elected officials have found that these types of laws are popular with their constituents, and they usually pass by large margins. Whereas it is no longer considered appropriate to bash other groups, gay men and lesbians are still fair game in courts and legislatures. However, if Hawaii ever does start issuing marriage licenses, the federal and state laws prohibiting same-sex marriages will begin to be challenged on federal and state constitutional grounds. Because of the high-profile nature of the *Baehr* case and subsequen' eral legislation, the current trends in this area cha. new rulings are made and new laws are passed.

THE SPREAD OF DOMESTIC PARTNERSHIP BENEFITS

Despite the lack of formal recognition for same-sex marriages, some governmental entities (such as city governments), public and private universities, and private businesses have extended domestic partnership benefits to gay men and lesbians and their partners. These benefits most often include health insurance coverage and, in some cases, bereavement and family medical leave. Some institutions have also extended the benefits to unmarried heterosexual couples.

Private Business Support for Domestic Partnership

In 1996, approximately two hundred companies extended benefits to same-sex domestic partners, making a total of approximately five hundred employers who provide such a benefit. However, these benefits do not protect gay men and lesbians and their partners in many difficult situations in which married heterosexual couples are granted automatic rights. Such situations include hospital visitation for an ill spouse or rights to a spouse's property after the spouse dies without a will. Thus domestic partnership benefits provide support to same-sex relationships in a narrow sphere, while in most other contexts gay men and lesbians continue to be treated as legal strangers.

Given the widespread governmental attacks on same-sex marriages, it seems ironic that businesses, which often are very conservative, should be leaders in recognizing the reality of gay and lesbian relationships. Several factors appear to be operative. For one, there may be more governmental resistance to altering the concept of *marriage*, which has deep religious meaning for many Americans, than to ensuring workplace equality through domestic partner benefits; thus acceptance of the more limited domestic partnership benefits does not necessarily mean acceptance of same-sex marriage. Second, companies have found that to attract top talent, which includes lesbian and gay employees, domestic benefits are important. In some industries (such as the computer industry), benefits plans have been adopted in a short time by most of the major companies in order to remain competitive, including Hewlett-Packard, IBM, Lotus, Microsoft, Apple, and others. Finally, from a more practical standpoint, companies have found that domestic partner benefits do not add much to benefits costs, and the increase in benefits enrollment has been less than 1 percent. Potential reasons for the low use of domestic partnership benefits include (1) fear of *coming out* (disclosing one's gay identity) at work; (2) the benefits that same-sex partners may already have at their own job may overlap with domestic partnership benefits; and (3) the tax increase that results from domestic partnership benefits, which are considered taxable income.

At least one state insurance commissioner (Georgia's John Oxendine) has ruled that private companies cannot offer domestic partnership benefits, even if both employer and employee wish to do so. This ruling not only runs counter to requests from various insurance companies that would like to offer the benefits; it also contradicts a legal opinion issued by the state attorney general. While large companies that are self-insured, such as IBM, American Express, Hewlett-Packard, and Lotus can offer domestic partnership benefits in Georgia under federal law, Georgia companies that purchase a group policy from an insurance company will not be able to choose the option of providing domestic partnership benefits. It is ironic (but not too surprising) that a free-market Republican would support this ultimate governmental intrusion into private enterprise. So far, no other state has taken this position.

Another controversy arose when "family"-oriented companies such as Walt Disney began offering domestic partnership benefits. Christian organizations have organized boycotts of Walt Disney films and theme parks to protest such actions, but the protests have yet to cause any company to retract its policy. The most recent high-profile organization to address domestic partner benefits issues was the Democratic National Committee, which announced in May 1997 that it was adding these benefits for its employees.

Public Sector Support for Domestic Partnership

As of September 1996, three states and fifty-two municipalities, school districts, or governmental entities have extended domestic partnership benefits to public employees. Attempts to provide these benefits have been challenged in court in some instances. For example, Atlanta passed an ordinance in 1993 to provide domestic partnership benefits to city employees, but it never went into effect; it was overturned by the Georgia Supreme Court because it classified domestic partners as "family." In 1996, a new ordinance was passed in Atlanta that called domestic partners "dependents" rather than "family" in an attempt to provide benefits in light of the court ruling. This new ordinance was promptly challenged in court by right-wing activists, and as of this writing the fate of the ordinance has not been decided.

In a unique twist on the road to same-sex marriage, public sector and private interests were merged by a City of San Francisco ordinance passed in November 1996 that required companies to provide spousal benefits to unmarried partners, regardless of their sex, as a condition of doing business with the city. Initially, there was some legal question about whether a city could force a national or international company to change its benefits. The law took effect on June 1, 1997, although some companies got extensions. A number of large companies examined their policies, and some, including Goodyear, the San Francisco 49ers football team, and the San Francisco Giants baseball team, have changed or plan to change to meet the requirements of the ordinance. We expect that the San Francisco ordinance will cause the number of private companies offering domestic partnership benefits to soar. In some cases, large companies have extended benefits nationwide based on this local ordinance.

Due to the San Francisco ordinance, in March 1997 Bank of America, the third largest bank in the United States, announced its intention to provide domestic partnership benefits. The Catholic Church, which has contracts with San Francisco worth $5.6 million a year through Catholic Charities, originally vehemently opposed the ordinance because it purportedly violated "religious and ethical tenets." However, a compromise was reached in early 1997 that will allow church employees to designate any one member of their household as eligible for "spousal-equivalent benefits." On the other hand, over twenty major airlines sued the city in May 1997, alleging that the city had overstepped its jurisdiction into matters dictated by federal law. The persistence of San Francisco Mayor Willie Brown assured that the ordinance would actually have its intended effect in most cases. Cities such as New York, Boston, and West Hollywood have since expressed interest in the possibility of implementing a similar ordinance. If this type of ordinance does spread, the possibility of legal challenges grows more likely.

CONCLUSION

As heterosexual Americans continue to learn more about gay men and lesbians, attitudes toward gay rights tend to change in a supportive direction. For example, as Americans have learned that gay men and lesbians can be fired in most states solely based on their sexual orientation, support for antidiscrimination legislation has soared above 70 percent. Similarly, since 1993, support for same-sex marriage has increased, although opposition is still above 50 percent in every poll. A postelection survey in late 1996 found support for recognizing same-sex relationships in the following situations: 46 percent for Social Security benefits, 52 percent for health care benefits, 62 percent for inheritance rights, and 82 percent for visitation rights. As the gay and lesbian community continues to educate friends, relatives, and co-workers about the reality of our lives, we move further down the road toward the full recognition of same-sex relationships.

References

Clay, R. A. (1997, February). Psychology informs debate on same-gender marriages. *American Psychological Association Monitor, 40.*

Curiel, J. (1997, March 18). The little city that could: Risking tens of millions of dollars, San Francisco forces big business to offer domestic partner benefits. *The Advocate, 28–31.*

Flaks, D. K., Ficher, I., Masterpasqua, F., & Joseph, G. (1995). Lesbians choosing motherhood: A comparative study of lesbian and heterosexual parents and their children. *Developmental Psychology, 31,* 105–114.

Gallagher, J. (1996, July 23). Love and war. *The Advocate,* 22–28.

Gallagher, J. (1997, February 4). Marriage, Hawaiian style. *The Advocate,* 22–28.

Gallagher, J. (1997, May 27). Marriage compromise. *The Advocate,* 71.

Golden, D. (1997, February 20). Still exposed: Oxendine's rule prohibits insurance companies from offering domestic partnership coverage in Georgia. *Southern Voice, 1,* 3–4.

Gover, T. (1997, January 21). For love or money: Despite the Hawaii ruling, the federal government still won't recognize gay marriage, leaving only corporate America to give us what's right: domestic-partner benefits. *The Advocate,* 22–28.

Herek, G. M. (1991). Myths about sexual orientation: A lawyer's guide to social science research. *Law and Sexuality: A Review of Lesbian and Gay Legal Issues, 1,* 133–172.

Kirkpatrick, M. (1996). Lesbians as parents. In R. P. Cabaj & T. S. Stein (Eds.), *Textbook of homosexuality and mental health* (pp. 353–370). Washington, DC: American Psychiatric Press.

Moss, J. J. (1995, October 15). Jilted: Gays and lesbians lost a battle over the right to marry, but not without protest. *The Advocate,* pp. 22–23, 27.

Patterson C. J. (1995). Lesbian mothers, gay fathers, and their children. In A. R. D'Augelli & C. J Patterson (Eds.), *Lesbian, gay, and bisexual identities over the lifespan: Psychological perspectives* (pp. 262–290). New York: Oxford University Press.

Patterson, C. J., & Chan, R. W. (1996). Gay fathers and their children. In R. P. Cabaj & T. S. Stein (Eds.), *Textbook of homosexuality and mental health* (pp. 371–393). Washington, DC: American Psychiatric Press.

Purcell, D. W., & Hicks D. W. (1996). Institutional discrimination against lesbians, gay men, and bisexuals: The courts, legislature, and the military. In R. P. Cabaj & T. S. Stein (Eds.), *Textbook of homosexuality and mental health.* Washington, DC: American Psychiatric Press.

Purdum, T. S. (1996, September 22). Gay rights groups attack Clinton on midnight signing. *New York Times,* p. 12.

Smith, D. M. (1997, Winter). HRC polls America: Trail-blazing surveys help accurately describe gay community, impact of our issues. *Human Rights Campaign Quarterly,* pp. 8–9.

Smothers, R. (1996, September 15). Lawsuit over Atlanta law on benefits for the unwed. *New York Times,* p. 13.

3

Lesbian Couples Creating Families

KATHRYN KENDELL

*This chapter reviews the direct impact that current
legal trends have on lesbians who are attempting to
form and maintain relationships and, especially, who
are seeking to create families that include children.
These same issues face gay men seeking to establish
their own families; but the majority of legal efforts
around same-sex couples and children have involved
lesbians. Without the legal protections that marriage
offers, many same-sex relationships, and the children
from them, will face undue hardships and possible
emotional disasters; hence the need for the option of
legal same-sex marriage and the reason why this road
is so important to take.*

Despite lack of legal recognition and protection, lesbians and
gay men have always formed intimate relationships, and
many of these families have included children. While the lack of
legal sanction for such families has presented untold hardship, the
growth in visibility of lesbian- and gay-headed households has made
obvious to much of the United States the second-class status these
families face. Few areas of law illustrate more clearly the harsh ramifications of the lack of legal recognition for lesbian and gay

41

relationships than matters involving children. This chapter focuses on the impact of the lack of legal marriage rights on lesbian couples and families.

CHILDREN WITHOUT THE BENEFIT OF MARRIAGE

It is estimated that six to fourteen million children are being raised in lesbian- or gay-headed households. Increasingly, lesbians are choosing to rear children through adoption or alternative forms of conception. For such families, our legal system's failure to recognize and protect the relationship of the parents creates vulnerability and marginalization. In everything from health insurance to hospital visitation or treatment, the inability of a lesbian couple to secure a legally recognizable relationship with each other and with their children often wreaks havoc. Moreover, for children who were conceived in a heterosexual marriage and who are now being raised by a lesbian mother, the threat is always present of a custody battle, instigated by the father, based solely on the mother's sexual orientation.

The Heterosexual Privilege of Automatic Protection

With few exceptions, U.S. family law is based on a two-parent heterosexual model. Under this model, families are automatically afforded enormous legal protections. The instant a heterosexual married couple gives birth, a legally recognized and protected relationship between the couple and their child is created. Both adults instantly become "parents," with all the legal and societal responsibilities and protections such a status carries.

This legal bond exists in most states even if the husband is not the biological father of the child. The only mechanism for severing this parental relationship, short of death, is through a judicial termination of parental rights based on unfitness or abandonment—a difficult, cumbersome, and unlikely possibility. As parents, both are legally and financially responsible for their children, and both have an equal right to make myriad decisions for and about their children, decisions that will not be disturbed or interfered with, unless harm to the child is demonstrated.

Lack of Protection for Lesbians and Their Children

For a lesbian couple the picture is markedly different. When a lesbian couple has a child, only the biological mother has any legally recognized relationship or rights. Regardless of how long the couple has been together or how committed the nonbiological parent, there is only one legal parent—the biological mother. Unless a lesbian couple adopts their child or children jointly or undergoes a second-parent adoption—both of which are granted only sporadically—their children lack significant protection. The child and the child's nonbiological parent have no legal connection to each other. The ramifications of such a fact can be startling.

To best illustrate the situation, let's imagine a lesbian couple, Jean and Debra. The couple, like thousands of lesbian-headed families, has two children by alternative insemination, ages seven and four. Debra is the biological mother of both. Let's assume that Jean and Debra have been together for twelve years. Jean is a lawyer, and Debra is a self-employed, part-time financial planner who works out of the couple's home.

Under this scenario, these two children have only one legally recognized mother—Debra. Jean, the primary breadwinner, cannot cover the children under her health insurance at work, because the children are not recognized as her dependents. If Jean were to die at the hands of a drunk driver, the children could not make a wrongful death claim or receive social security survivor's benefits. If Jean did not have the foresight to make a will, neither Debra nor the children would have a legal claim to any of Jean's assets. If Jean had no documents indicating her funeral wishes, Debra would have no right to make any decisions regarding death arrangements, such as burial or cremation, even if she and Jean discussed the matter informally. Both Debra and the children are regarded as legal strangers to Jean, with no rights whatsoever. Jean's biological family, regardless of where they live or the nature of her relationship with them, would have the right to all the assets of the estate and the right to make all decisions.

If Debra were to die, the situation would be even worse. Because Jean has no legally recognized relationship with the children, she may be denied custody of them, regardless of the length of her parental relationship, her parental ability, Debra's wishes, or the wishes of the children. If a family member, no matter how distant, were to sue for custody, Jean might well lose the children or, at the very least, be embroiled in a long legal battle.

If the couple were to separate, Jean would be under no legal obligation to pay child support or alimony. While many lesbian partners assume these obligations out of a moral sense of responsibility, some do not. In such cases, the children or family suffers and may in fact need state assistance. Moreover, because Jean has no legally enforceable right to visitation, Debra may successfully deny Jean any contact with the children in the event of a split. Each of the foregoing scenarios is possible because family law in the United States fully recognizes only one type of family: the family headed by a heterosexual, legally married couple. The ramifications of second-class status for lesbian- and gay-headed families can be seen in one heartbreaking case after another.

Legal Cases Affecting Lesbian-Headed Households

In Oregon, a lesbian couple had been together for eight years raising the two children they had through alternative insemination. Tragically, the biological mother died in a car accident in 1990. The parents of the biological mother sued the surviving parent for custody, despite the fact that the children had only incidental contact with their grandparents. Fortunately, the trial court denied the grandparents petition for custody but only after substantial emotional upheaval for the children and their only surviving parent. In Florida, a similar situation occurred, but the grandparents prevailed in receiving the custody award and having an adoption petition granted with no notice to the surviving parent. Finally, the adoption was overturned on appeal, and in 1992 the children were awarded back to the only other parent they had ever known.

In 1993, Mary Ward, a lesbian mother in Pensacola, Florida, lost custody of her youngest daughter to her ex-husband, who had served eight years in prison for murdering his first wife. Mary lost custody because the court found that her lesbian "lifestyle" rendered her less able to adequately care for her daughter than the girl's father, who had recently remarried, in the judge's words, a "good woman."

The Florida Appellate Court affirmed the trial court ruling, agreeing that there was evidence of detriment and harm that would continue if the child stayed with her mother. The "evidence" consisted of testimony from the father that the child had poor hygiene, preferred men's cologne, and asked questions about adult relationships. From these "facts" the court determined that the child was exposed to inappropriate behavior in her mother's care. While motions for rehearing were pending in January of 1997, Mary Ward died suddenly from a heart attack, leaving her partner of four years and their four children—including her daughter—at the center of the custody dispute. She also lost the opportunity to call for an examination of a court ruling that clearly applied a double standard when dealing with lesbian and, presumably, gay parents.

In 1991, Sharon Bottoms was challenged for custody of her four-year-old son, Tyler, by Sharon's mother, Kay. Kay sought custody based on her assertion that Sharon's "lesbian lifestyle" was detrimental to the young boy. After losing custody of her son at the trial court level, Sharon appealed to the Virginia Court of Appeals, which reversed the trial court and found that there was no evidence that Tyler had been harmed by his mother's sexual orientation. Kay then appealed to the Virginia Supreme Court. In a split opinion, the court ruled that there was evidence of harm sufficient to render

Sharon unfit for custody. While the court found Sharon unfit based on employment factors and other factors unrelated to sexual orientation, it also made clear that being gay or lesbian was itself sufficient grounds for denying custody because of the "social condemnation" and stigma that the child would have to suffer.

While the Virginia Supreme Court opinion pretends not to unduly consider the issue of Sharon's sexual orientation, it is clear that if Sharon had not been a lesbian, custody of her son would never have been threatened. If Sharon's relationship with her partner, April, had been a neutral issue or even a fact in her favor, as is the case with most heterosexual marriages, her son would still be with her today.

If the couples in each of these cases had been in relationships respected and protected by the legal system, none of these tragic stories would have taken place. The surviving partners in Oregon and Florida would have automatically been fully recognized as the children's legal surviving parent. Mary Ward would never have lost custody in the first place, because she would have been in a relationship that carried the same legal standing as her ex-husband's new marriage. More importantly, Mary Ward's partner would have been entitled to visitation rights upon Mary's death. And Sharon Bottoms, her partner, and her son would be living together as an intact family.

The foregoing stories are not isolated or uncommon. They occur with alarming frequency around the country. They are stories every lesbian has heard many times. They are the stories that reinforce that lesbian and gay families are not just "less than" in theory but in brutal practice.

Battling the Myths

The lack of legally protected and sanctioned relationships permits myths about lesbian parents to persist. Legal marriage would not instantly erase ignorance and homophobia any more than *Brown v. Board of Education*, the landmark school desegregation case, erased

racism. But legal status for lesbian and gay relationships would sig-
nal that such myths no longer are legally permitted to influence
and fuel social attitudes or judicial decision making. In virtually
every case in which a lesbian loses custody or visitation with her
children or has her relationship with her partner denigrated, the
justification for such a conclusion includes a litany of the supposed
harms lesbian mothers inflict upon their children. These harm alle-
gations are based on easily refutable but persistent myths about lesbian mothers.

The most common myths include the view that children raised
by lesbian or gay parents will grow up gay themselves; that children
will by psychologically damaged; that they will be overly eroticized
or sexualized; or that they will be mercilessly harassed and ostracized.
While repeated social science studies demonstrate that none of these
common myths has any factual basis, judges, policy makers, and many
Americans continue to routinely invoke such untruths to deny legal
recognition and protection to lesbian families.

Often these justifications appear in judicial opinions that are
completely unsupported by any authority. The bias persists because
it can: because lesbian parents have no legally protected status,
opinions based solely on prejudice are not just tolerated but allowed
to flourish. In the Mary Ward case, the trial court judge noted that
he was denying Mary custody in order to ensure that her daughter
grew up in a "nonlesbian world." The judge continued, "As this
young girl approaches womanhood she should not be led into a
lifestyle which she would not ordinarily choose."

In another lesbian mother custody case in Florida in 1996,
despite the testimony of a respected psychologist that the mother's
sexual orientation created no negative effects on the child and was
irrelevant to her parenting ability, the trial court judge ruled that
he was taking "judicial notice" of the fact that being raised by a lesbian mother would cause grave harm. The myths live on in spite of
overwhelming evidence to the contrary. Of the dozens of studies
done on children of lesbian parents, all confirm the same result: that

sexual orientation is irrelevant to parental ability. As David Flaks, in a recent summary of this research, concluded, "The social science literature . . . demonstrates clearly that lesbians and gay men can and do raise psychologically healthy children. In fact, no evidence . . . suggests that homosexual parents are inferior to their heterosexual counterparts, or that their children are in any regard compromised." And, as Chapter Five points out, every credible study concludes that our children are as psychologically healthy and adjusted as children who are raised in heterosexual households. Certainly, not all lesbians or gay men are good parents, any more than all heterosexuals are good parents; but the sexual orientation of a parent does not in any way determine whether he or she will be a proper parent.

Ensuring that such conclusions have force of law has been painstakingly slow, and the process is made even more difficult by the marginal legal position of lesbian families.

JANE V. JANE: THE DOUBLE STANDARD OF INTRACOMMUNITY BATTLES

Disrespect, lack of legal recognition, internalized homophobia, and, perhaps, human nature sometimes coalesce to present some of the most wrenching family battles among gay- and lesbian-headed families. As more and more lesbian couples have children, inevitable breakups of some couples lead, sadly, to some of the very same visitation or custody disputes seen in the heterosexual context. And where a lesbian couple uses a known semen donor to assist in creating their family, a new area of conflict has developed when the expectations of the donor and the lesbian couple diverge.

Unfortunately, lesbian families have none of the automatic protections accorded heterosexual couples. So the battles reflect power that favors biology, regardless of the family structure or intent of the parties when they were still an intact family.

Donor-Insemination Cases

Time and again the legal system demonstrates inflexibility and inability to justly resolve conflicts or challenges facing lesbian-headed households. Most often the legal system defaults to patriarchal notions of family never intended by the lesbian couple. For example if our hypothetical couple, Jean and Debra, used a known semen donor in the creation of their children, the potential for conflict and complication increases exponentially. My purpose is not to discourage women and men from entering into alternative and inclusive family structures but to point out that current law has not manifested the flexibility to honor such alternative families in the event of disagreement. Obviously, for every contested situation involving a known donor there are thousands that proceed without conflict.

The problem in many cases involving known donors is that the donor is legally determined to be the father in the event of a dispute between him and the couple. Such a conclusion has been reached by courts even where the evidence is clear that neither the lesbian couple nor the donor intended that he be considered a parent. Many lesbian couples choose to create families through arrangements with sperm donors who will be known to the child and who will have some involvement in the child's life. In most cases the donor, by verbal or written agreement, is not regarded as a parent by the parties but rather as a "special friend" or man who "helped make" the child. Regardless of the parties' intent to not recognize the donor as a legally or emotionally involved parent, many courts refuse to honor the intent of the parties and instead have ruled that the donor's status as the biological progenitor of the child trumps any stated or contractual intent of the parties. This biology-is-destiny mentality denies alternative family structures and certainly devalues planned lesbian families.

Several cases illustrate this approach. In the first reported California case involving a lesbian couple, a semen donor successfully sued for paternity of a child who was nine months old at the time the action was commenced. At the time of the insemination in *Jhordan C.*, California had adopted a statute whereby a donor of semen provided to a licensed physician for use in artificial insemination would not be regarded by law as the child's natural father. The parties had conducted the insemination without a physician. The failure to avail themselves of the statute and the disputed understanding of the parties regarding the involvement of the donor resulted in the court approving the donor claim to paternity. In a subsequent California case, the donor again was issued an order of paternity. Here, the lesbian couple again did not avail themselves of the statute, and the facts recounted by the parties as to their intent and course of conduct differed dramatically.

If the cases ended here, one could conclude that contested facts, a history of contacts, and the failure to invoke statutory protections, rather than a reflexive reliance on biology, lead to the courts' failure to honor lesbian family structures. Unfortunately, a 1996 case addressing a contested donor claim to paternity belies such a conclusion. In *Thomas S.* v. *Robin Y.*, a known donor's petition for paternity was granted by a New York State appellate court. The court, reversing the ruling of the family court below, held that Thomas S. was entitled to an order of filiation (paternity) despite facts that demonstrated that his contacts with the child had been sporadic and always within the control of the child's mothers. At the time the child was conceived no statute terminating a donor's rights existed in New York, and neither Thomas S. nor Robin Y. knew about the California statute. The appellate court held that the existence of the statute was not relevant to the outcome in this case. The court ruled that an order of filiation was proper, in part, largely because Thomas S. was "conceded to be a biological father"; thus his "parental rights" could not be "terminated absent proper procedures." In this case, biology became the court's focus rather than the reality of the parties' intent and the child's view of her family.

This series of cases demonstrates that the legal system's notion of "family" continues to be a male-female, father-mother model, with biology reigning supreme. The inflexibility of the legal system, particularly to respond to the reality of lesbian families, is a primary reason legal marriage for lesbian couples has such an attraction, even with the flaws of marriage as an institution.

Planned lesbian families are not recognized as "real" families by most courts. Courts cannot seem to avoid giving biology a primacy never contemplated by the parties initially, and donors cannot seem to avoid invoking biology as the mantel for staking a parental claim they previously eschewed. Under our current legal system it is the status of marriage alone that automatically confers the whole panoply of rights to families and their children.

Lesbian Visitation Cases

Under heterosexual family law, a father or mother is absolutely entitled to visitation upon divorce, unless such visitation poses harm to the child. But for lesbian families, unless the couple got a second-parent adoption, the nonbiological parent is treated as a stranger who must fight in court to prove she fulfilled a parental role. Once she does that, the nonbiological mother may still not get any visitation, particularly if the biological parent objects. In other words, the law does not recognize a lesbian family as one to which the conventional legal rules apply. Perhaps most distressing, the biological parent is often a willing co-conspirator in this exclusion and use of homophobic reasoning.

Family law issues involving lesbians and gay men used to be confined solely to a lesbian mother losing custody of her child to a heterosexual ex-husband. However, the issues of the 1990s are just as likely to be intracommunal as they are intercommunal. As with the progression of any movement, lesbians have moved from fighting exclusively with ex-husbands and homophobic judges to battling ex-partners and a legal system that fails to recognize our families. The situation is all too familiar. A couple lives together in relationship for many years; they choose to have children. One of them becomes pregnant, and they both participate in raising their child. The couple splits up. The biological parent then denies the nonbiological parent visitation with the child (or children) they raised together.

While the donor cases and lesbian-visitation cases have marked differences, the core arguments are strikingly similar, based on a universal disrespect for and diminution of the importance of lesbian couples and their children as creating a freestanding, fully functioning family. The general assumptions underlying all the arguments are that these families are not real, are not worthy of recognition and respect, and do not warrant a legal analysis consistent with what would be accorded to a heterosexual couple and their children.

The fact that arguments for dismantling lesbian-headed families come from within the lesbian community and often rely on arguments against same-sex relationships in general is particularly distressing and reflects win-at-all-costs thinking. The mentality is not only disruptive but ultimately plays into the hands of those opposed to lesbian and gay families generally, who assert that our families do not matter and, in fact, should not exist with any support, protections, or encouragement.

In J.A.L. v. E.P.H, a Pennsylvania appellate court in 1996 ruled that J.A.L., the nonbiological parent, had acted as and been treated as a parent and was entitled to petition a court for visitation with her daughter. Despite facts that demonstrated that the biological mother intended J.A.L. to be the child's co-parent and that J.A.L. had performed as a parent since the child's birth, she was denied standing to make a claim for visitation by the trial court. On appeal, the appellate court reversed and granted standing concluding that J.A.L. had clearly demonstrated her role as a parent to her daughter. Courts in Wisconsin, Utah, and New Mexico have rendered decisions similar to that of the appellate court in Pennsylvania. In each successful case the court thoroughly reviewed the facts, which demonstrated that the nonbiological or adoptive parent functioned as a parent and assumed parental responsibilities.

While some courts have ruled in favor of co-parent claims, thereby allowing the co-parent to petition for visitation with her child, many courts have reached the opposite conclusion. An appellate court in California ruled in 1989 that a lesbian co-parent was essentially a biological stranger who was not entitled to make any claim for visitation, despite co-parenting two children for over eight years. Recent decisions in New Hampshire and Vermont have also denied standing to lesbian co-parents.

SECOND-CLASS SOLUTIONS

Despite the lack of substantive legal protections for lesbian- or gay-headed families, there have been some piecemeal gains in securing legal recognition. The most promising mechanism for lesbians or gay men with children allows a nonbiological coparent to petition as a legally recognized adoptive parent, now an actual reality in some courts.

Second-Parent Adoption

Second-parent adoption is an important way for lesbian and gay couples to secure legal recognition and protection of their families. For over a decade, such adoptions have been granted by the thousands in California. As of this writing, trial or appellate courts in seventeen states have granted such adoptions.

The phrase *second-parent adoption* first appeared in the family law literature in 1986. A second-parent adoption arises primarily in the context of a lesbian relationship and, to a lesser extent, in gay male relationships. In each case, one partner in the relationship is a biological or adoptive parent of a child or children. The couple desires to have the nonbiological, nonadoptive parent recognized as a legal parent. The nonbiological parent petitions the court to grant her status as a legal parent through a second-parent adoption (also referred to as *limited-consent adoption*). The process is very similar in concept to a stepparent adoption. Unlike in a conventional adoption, in a second-parent adoption the rights and obligations of the child's biological parent are not terminated.

This mechanism is certainly not a panacea, nor is it a satisfying substitute for legal marriage. While such an adoption does provide a child with two legally recognized parents and does allow a child to receive substantial economic benefits and security, the process does nothing to legally protect the relationship between the two parents with each other. Moreover, the option of second-parent adoption remains unavailable in many states where individual judges would be hostile to such a prospect. In 1994, the Wisconsin State Supreme Court held that such adoptions could not be permitted under that court's literal reading of the state adoption statute. Recently, the Colorado Court of Appeal likewise held that second-parent adoptions were not allowed by the terms of that state's adoption statute. When it comes to second-parent adoptions, the happenstance of geography may well determine the level of legal recognition and protection afforded lesbian families.

Other Solutions

Like the silver-lining of second-parent adoptions, there have been a handful of developments that indicate some loosening of the strict heterosexual model of a family. Dozens of municipalities and hundreds of companies extend some form of domestic partner benefits to their employees. Recent court decisions have allowed gay or lesbian "spouses" to claim family status for purposes of rent-controlled housing. Many varied religious denominations sanction and perform same-sex "union ceremonies" for lesbian and gay couples. And, of course, lesbian and gay visibility is at an all-time high.

Certainly, these developments increase our ability to create and sustain lesbian families. But the shortcomings in such promising beginnings is palpable. If we assume that Jean and Debra, our hypothetical lesbian couple, live in a place where second-parent adoption is possible, if Jean has domestic partner benefits available where she works, if their neighbors and families are supportive, if their church minister celebrates their union and family—all this support notwithstanding, Debra and Jean are legally marginalized. Our legal system has created a caste status whereby sexual orientation alone is the delineator between families who receive a wealth of benefits and protections and families who must struggle with a fraction of what is automatically provided to others.

CONCLUSION

The battle by lesbians and gay men for the right to marry is fundamentally about not only justice and equality but family stability and security. The failure of the American legal system to protect our alternative family structures results in real, measurable harm to our relationships and our children. As long as our legal system imbues the status of marriage with so many rights and protections, and as long as this system wholly fails to honor lesbian-headed families, legal marriage provides the only option not just for civil equality but for the most basic and rudimentary protections.

References

Alpert, H. (1988). *We are everywhere: Writings by and about lesbian parents*. Freedom, CA: Crossing Press.

Belcastro, P. A., Gramlich, T., Price, J., & Wilson, R. (1993). A review of data based studies addressing the effects of homosexual parenting on children's sexual and social functioning. *Journal of Divorce and Remarriage, 20,* 105–122.

Benkov, L. (1994). *Reinventing the family: The emerging story of lesbian and gay parents*. New York: Crown.

Bigner, J. J., & Bozett, F. W. (1990). Parenting by gay fathers. In F. W. Bozett & M. B. Sussman (Eds.), *Homosexuality and family relations* (pp. 155–176). New York: Harrington Park Press.

Bozett, F. W. (1987). *Gay and lesbian parents*. New York: Praeger.

Bozett, F. W. (1990). A review of the literature. In F. W. Bozett & M. B. Sussman (Eds.), *Homosexuality and family relations* (pp. 137–162). New York: Harrington Park Press.

Clunis, D. M., & Green, G. D. (1988). Lesbian couples with children. In D. M. Clunis & G. D. Green (Eds.), *Lesbian couples* (pp. 113–130). Seattle, WA: Seal Press.

Cramer, D. (1986). Gay parents and their children: A review of research and practical implications. *Journal of Counseling and Development, 64*, 504–507.

Falk, P. J. (1994). The gap between psychosocial assumptions and empirical research in lesbian-mother child custody cases. In A. E. Gottfried & A. W. Gottfried (Eds.), *Redefining families: Implications for children's development* (pp. 131–156). New York: Plenum.

Flaks, D. K. (1994). Lesbian families: Judicial assumptions, scientific realities. *William and Mary Bill of Rights Journal, 3*, 345–371.

Gil de Lamadrid, M. (Ed.). (1991). *Lesbians choosing motherhood: Legal implications of donor insemination and co-parenting*. San Francisco: National Center for Lesbian Rights.

Golombok, S., Spencer, A., & Rutter, M. (1983). Children in lesbian and single-parent households: Psychosexual and psychiatric appraisal. *Journal of Child Psychology and Psychiatry, 24*, 551–572.

Gottman, J. S. (1990). Children of gay and lesbian parents. In F. W. Bozett & M. B. Sussman, (Eds.), *Homosexuality and family relations* (pp. 177–196). New York: Harrington Park Press.

Green, R., Mandel, J. B., Gotvedt, M. E., Gray, J., & Smith, L. (1986). Lesbian mothers and their children: A comparison with solo parent heterosexual mothers and their children. *Archives of Sexual Behavior, 15*, 167–184.

Herek, G. M. (1991). Myths about sexual orientation: A lawyer's guide to social science research. *Law and Sexuality, 1*, 133–172.

Kleber, D. J., Howell, R. J., & Tibbits-Kleber, A. L. (1986). The impact of parental homosexuality in child custody cases: A review of the literature. *Bulletin of the American Academy of Psychiatry and Law, 14*, 81–87.

Lyons, T. A. (1983). Lesbian mothers' custody fears. *Women and Therapy, 2*, 231–240.

Martin, A. (1989). The planned lesbian and gay family: Parenthood and children. *Newsletter of the Society for the Psychological Study of Lesbian and Gay Issues, 5*, 6 & 16–17.

Martin, A. (1993). *The lesbian and gay parenting handbook*. New York: Harper-Collins.

National Association of Social Workers. (1994). Policy statement on lesbian and gay issues. *Social work speaks: NASW policy statements* (pp. 162–165). Washington, DC: National Association of Social Workers.

Patterson, C. J. (1992). Children of lesbian and gay parents. *Child Development, 63,* 1025–1042.

Patterson, C. J. (1994). Lesbian and gay families. *Current Directions in Psychological Science, 3,* 62–64.

Pies, C. (1985). *Considering parenthood: A workbook for lesbians.* San Francisco: Spinsters Ink.

Polikoff, N. (1986). Lesbian mothers, lesbian families: Legal obstacles, legal challenges. *Review of Law and Social Change, 14(4),* 907–914.

Schulenberg, J. (1985). *Gay parenting: A complete guide for gay men and lesbians with children.* New York: Anchor Books.

Weston, K. (1991). *Families we choose: Lesbians, gays, kinship.* New York: Columbia University Press.

4

Gay Male Couples and Families

MICHAEL BETTINGER

Same-sex couples have had many psychological and legal issues to face over the years to establish and maintain their relationships. Though this chapter focuses on the path that gay male relationships have taken, most of the issues are also relevant for lesbian couples. The emotional impact of marriage—the need to have love acknowledged—applies to all couples. Successfully maneuvering down the road to same-sex marriage requires a full understanding of the emotional and psychological issues facing couples and the possible impact of legally sanctioned relationships.

As the right for people of the same sex to marry legally becomes increasingly probable, it is perhaps time to speculate on the impact this will have on same-sex couples. The legal aspects of such marriages are examined elsewhere in this book. The ability to marry someone of the same sex will, however, have a profound impact, both emotional and practical, on gay people as

Note: All of the gay men used as examples in this chapter are friends or acquaintances of this author; their names and some identifying characteristics have been changed to protect their identities.

individuals, as couples, and, in increasing numbers, as members of multigenerational families created by gay couples. Also affected will be the families of origin of those couples and the community and society in which the couples live. This impact will be different depending upon whether couples decide to avail themselves of or refrain from their option to marry legally.

THE INSTITUTION OF MARRIAGE AND GAY PEOPLE

Marriage and family are institutions that will continue to evolve as long as humans mate. In ancient times, the patriarchs of the Bible had polygamous marriages as did the Mormons in the nineteenth century, when marriage and family were patriarchal institutions.

For many today, heterosexual marriage and family remain firmly rooted in the patriarchal model. Christian men's groups, such as The Promise Keepers, hold rallies in baseball stadiums filled to capacity to remind Christian husbands of their responsibly to be the head of the home and family. For others, however, heterosexual marriage appears to be evolving toward an egalitarian model, especially among younger adults.

Until the 1960s, marriage between African Americans and European Americans was illegal in many states. Marriages arranged by the parents of a couple were common in this country in the nineteenth century, and are still common in many parts of the world. Yet today in the United States, such arrangements would be considered antiquated and possibly abusive of the rights and happiness of the couple.

Our concept of marriage and family has changed and continues to change. Only recently has it become possible to include gay and lesbian couples in the evolving model of marriage and family because until the twentieth century, people did not understand that men and women were not only divided by sex but were also divided by sexual orientation. It was generally believed that effeminate men who displayed homosexual desires were *fairies*, defective men who were acting like women. It was possible for a "normal" man to have sex with a fairy and not be considered anything but heterosexual, because fairies were like women. We now understand that sexual orientation is an independent variable apart from gender or biological sex, and thus we can include same-sex couples in our understanding of healthy ways people mate.

Gay male relationships are also evolving. Being marginalized by society, gay men have developed relationships in a world separate from heterosexual relationships. In some ways, the relationships of gay men are similar to the relationships of heterosexuals, but in other ways gay male relationships are unique. They differ not only from heterosexual but also from lesbian relationships. The impact of legal same-sex marriage on gay men will also be different from its impact on lesbians.

To understand the probable impact of legal marriage specifically on gay male couples, it will be necessary to have a general understanding of what gay male couples are like. One cannot use heterosexual men or couples as examples and assume that legal marriage will have the same meaning and impact for gay male couples. Finally, it will also be important to understand the impact of legal marriage on families created by gay male couples.

HOW GAY AND NONGAY MEN DIFFER

The differences between gay male and heterosexual relationships come from three factors: (1) gay men are different from nongay men; (2) relationships between two people of the same sex have different dynamics than relationships between people of different sexes; and (3) gay male relationships, for the most part, develop out of sight from the nongay world and take different forms than nongay relationships.

It should come as no surprise that gay and nongay men have both differences and similarities. In our society, there has been a we-are-all-the-same mentality, whether it related to sexual orientation, race, or ethnicity. While we may be all inherently equal, we are not all alike. Gay men and straight men are more alike than different, but there are important differences.

Gay men, in general, are likely to be more androgynous than nongay men. *Androgyny* can be defined as the state where a person combines many of the personality characteristics traditionally seen as both male and female. This difference between gay and nongay men significantly affects the relationships that are formed by such gay men. Androgyny does not mean that a man who is androgynous is like a woman; gay men are not like women. Many gay men, however, incorporate significant personality traits usually associated with women, including greater sensitivity, empathy, and stronger orientation toward relationships.

Such differences do not suddenly appear in adulthood. Kinsey Institute researchers Bell, Weinberg, and Hammersmith report that gays and nongays were quite different even in childhood. Boys who grow up to be gay often did not conform to the gender roles usually assigned to little boys. Other writers also have noted that in many ways, gay men when they were children did not act in the ways we have come to expect little boys to act.

Boys who do not conform to expected gender behavior are often called sissies because of their lack of interest in sports and rough play and their greater interest in activities usually associated with young girls, such as playing house, reading, or being interested in the arts, dance, or quiet activities. The interest in playing house is telling; while many of their nongay siblings were interested in competitive activities, boys who grow up to be gay were often more interested in relationship activities.

As adults, gay men are often more sensitive, empathic, and generally better able to converse with women about marriage and relationship concerns. Gay men are probably overrepresented in professions where sensitivity is needed, everything from the arts to acting, hairdressing, teaching, or psychotherapy. While these traits do not represent all adult gay men or children who grow up to be gay, researchers have documented that they were present for many children who grew up to be gay and have affected their personalities as they grow older.

In their approach to sexuality, gay men are similar to heterosexual men, though the sex of their desired partner is different. Both usually are interested in sex with various partners and have the ability to separate sex from romance and intimacy. There are many individual exceptions for both gay and nongay men but, overall, gay men seem quite different from nongay men in relation to intimacy and relationships and strikingly similar to each other in regard to sexuality.

THE RELATIONSHIPS OF GAY MEN

Only one-third of all Americans have a friend, relative, or close acquaintance whom they know to be gay or lesbian. Accordingly, most people have no direct experience with gay relationships, and therefore myths abound.

Popular Myths about Gay Relationships

People unfamiliar with gay male relationships have at times assumed that gay male relationships are similar to heterosexual relationships regarding gender role expectations. In this model of relationships, one man is the masculine role partner and assumes the responsibilities usually associated with men, and the other is the feminine role partner, acting out the traditional female responsibilities.

While evidence indicates that this model of gay male relationships occurs infrequently, the myth of its commonality stubbornly endures. The extremely popular 1996 movie *The Birdcage* has actors Nathan Lane and Robin Williams portraying an older gay couple. Lane is feminine, weak, submissive, and ditzy; Williams is masculine, strong, dominant, and grounded. Lane is in charge of the home; Williams is in charge of the business. Lane is, in effect, the woman, and Williams is, of course, the man. Such a strict dichotomy of personality traits and work assignments in gay relationships does exist but is rare.

People probably believe this model of gay male couples because, as stated earlier, until this century, the only gay men that were widely known were the extremely effeminate gay men, or fairies, and the only gay couples were those composed of a "normal man" and a fairy. We are now able to conceptualize that two men (or two women), regardless of their outward masculinity or femininity, might want to be a couple, whereas this would have been exceedingly difficult for most people to understand in the past.

A second model of gay relationships, also mistakenly believed to exist commonly, is one in which there is a great age difference between the two men, with the older man dominating the younger man. The model is probably derived from two concepts. One concept is the idealized ancient Greek model of a relationship between an older and a younger man, where an older man becomes the mentor of a younger man and has a sexual relationship with him.

The second concept is rooted in a deep-seated prejudice and incorrect belief that gay men are pedophiles by nature and are intent on seeking out younger men to molest and convert to homosexuality. While older-younger gay relationships do exist, they probably occur as commonly as in heterosexual relationships and for the same reasons. Youth and beauty are prized in our society by some older men, both gay and nongay; they place a high value on youth and beauty in finding a mate, male or female.

The Prevalent Model of Gay Relationships

The most typical kind of gay male relationship is based on an egalitarian or best-friend model: the two men are roughly the same age and often of the same socioeconomic class. There is no clear dominant partner. Decision making is expected to be a shared process of two equals. While not always achieved, this is the form of relationship desired by most gay men and lesbians. In this model, not only is decision making expected to be equal but chores are also expected to be shared, although there will obviously be some division of labor based on individual preferences. Unlike heterosexual marriages, where the women may do the bulk of the housework, gay couples are likely to share the tasks roughly equally. When equality is not achieved, it is often the older one or the one with the higher income who dominates.

Flexibility is the hallmark of these relationships. While one partner might gravitate toward many of the activities usually associated with the male or female role, such role play is often not rigid. The one who does the laundry and dishes might also be the same one who fixes the car. The rules of such relationships need to be agreed upon either implicitly or explicitly, since many different types of egalitarian models of relationships exist within the gay male community.

Sexuality and Stable Relationships

The expression of sexuality in gay male relationships often needs to be determined by the couple. When two gay men decide to have a committed relationship, there is not an automatically accepted understanding that the relationship will be monogamous, non-monogamous, or even sexual. While these relationships are often quite close emotionally and usually marked by great flexibility, the rules regarding sexuality can differ widely between couples.

The apparent heterosexual standard is monogamy, and heterosexuals who have open relationships are usually regarded negatively. The gay male community has prided itself on its ability to accept a variety of nontraditional relationships, including open relationships (both acknowledged and tacit), menages (where more than two people are involved), and even nonsexual lovers who live together, identify as a couple, and are each other's primary emotional support and best friends but who also seek others for their sexual needs. Kinsey Institute surveys conducted by Bell and Weinberg divided gay men in relationships into sexually "open coupled" and "closed coupled," while Silverstein varied it by dividing gay men into categories of "excitement seekers" and "home builders," but those researchers noted that these conceptions left out many gay men. Moreover, there is some evidence that there has been an increase in monogamous gay relationships since the AIDS epidemic began in the 1980s.

Gay men also have stable long-term relationships in which the men do not live with each other. For a variety of reasons, two men might maintain separate households but be in a committed relationship. Other variations exist: sometimes one of the men remains legally married to a woman and continues living with her and their children, while maintaining a committed relationship with a man.

As the 1996 movie *The Celluloid Closet* portrayed, on those rare occasions when Hollywood depicted a gay man or couple in a film, the men were historically portrayed as silly, frivolous, criminal, unhappy, or even demented people in a sick relationship that almost always ended with the rejection, humiliation, arrest, imprisonment, hospitalization, suicide, murder, or death of one or both of the men. Hollywood seemed to believe that gay men could not have happy, loving, satisfying relationships. In reality, gay men and lesbians have been found to be as satisfied with their relationships as are heterosexuals.

The Development of Gay Relationships

The committed relationships of gay men are notable in how little they differ from heterosexual relationships. Commonly, gay men meet, fall in love, spend time together, set up a home, grow closer, merge money and possessions, learn to more deeply accept each other, build a life together and separate from each other, and finally lose a partner to death. Much like the family life cycle of heterosexuals, gay couples go through identifiable stages in their relationships, although differences also abound. Whereas heterosexuals usually marry someone quite similar to themselves in socioeconomic terms, gays relationships appear to be considerably more diverse on this dimension.

Like heterosexuals, where one out of two marriages end not with the death of a partner but with divorce, some gays also have a difficult time staying in relationships. Because there is no legal same-sex marriage, comparable statistics are difficult to obtain. Legal same-sex marriage might help us to understand why some gay relationships fail and thus help other gay couples to stay together, because it would be easier to identify those couples whose partnership did not last.

Satisfaction and Intimacy

Research over the past twenty years has resulted in a wealth of knowledge about gay relationships, which were not previously studied. We do now know that happiness in gay relationships appears to be related to many factors, just as it is in heterosexual marriages. When the rewards of the relationship outweigh the costs, the gay partners appear to be happier and more likely to stay together. Spending a lot of time together, merging money and finances, and having a satisfying sexual life all correlate with longevity in gay couples. Lack of time together, limited communication and support, or one partner having a serious problem, such as substance abuse, are factors in relationships less likely to endure.

Gay relationships in general are marked by greater emotional closeness than heterosexual relationships. *Closeness* here means asking each other for help, having friends in common, spending time on activities together, feeling emotionally intimate, having common interests, making decisions together, and valuing togetherness as a top priority. These traits are not the values or expectations of the heterosexual patriarchal model, although obviously there is a wide diversity among heterosexual couples.

It is possible that external factors drive gay couples closer together. Gay couples may receive little support from or even rejection by the general society, their families, religious institutions, and their employers. The only places gay men consistently may get support is from their mates, their friends, and the institutions created in the gay community. The lack of external support, along with the more androgynous nature of gay men, add up to a situation where gay men in relationships often turn to each other for closeness and support—as two against the world.

Lesbian and gay relationships exhibit significantly more flexibility than traditional heterosexual relationships, with lesbians being significantly more flexible than both gays and heterosexuals. While heterosexual roles in marriage are strongly linked to biological sex, gays and lesbians need to determine who does what each time they get into a relationship. Flexibility, thus, is needed for the relationships to succeed.

These factors—the greater desire for closeness, a rejecting world that drives gay men together, and the similarity between gay and nongay men's sexual needs—begin to shape the relationships that are formed. When those factors are combined with the greater flexibility needed in unsanctioned relationships between two people of the same sex, we see how these relationships differ from traditional heterosexual arrangements.

WHY PEOPLE SEEK RELATIONSHIPS

One of the most basic of human desires, regardless of sexual orientation, is the desire to find a mate. Much of the literature and stories in the oral traditions of most cultures—whether Western or Eastern, modern or primitive—contain the same theme: the desire to find a mate, the person with whom one wants to share one's life. Not only humans but the mythic gods and the subhuman creatures described in many cultures actively pursue finding their mate. From the time we are young, it is assumed we will grow up and marry.

Love and Happiness

We live in a society that seems to emphasize love above all else, and love and happiness are strongly associated. We are told the best reason for choosing a partner is romantic, sexual love of that person;

all other reasons may be denigrated. However, choosing a mate at other times and in other cultures was often about economic or political alliances between families. Marriages were often arranged. Stories of meeting a husband or wife for the first time at the altar were not uncommon. The current emphasis on love is reinforced by Christianity, which tells us love is the way to divine grace. In the words of the Beatles, "All you need is love."

Intimacy—that ephemeral yet enduring state where love, tenderness, erotic attraction, emotional closeness, intellectual sharing, and affection mix with companionship, a stable sexuality, and creation or extension of family—is emphasized as a goal from the time we are quite young. Love and a meaningful intimate connection is generally accepted as that which will make a difference in happiness in a person's life. A poor person dying surrounded by a loving family is considered by many to have had a better life than a rich person who dies alone, estranged from family or friends.

Gay Men Seeking Protected Relationships

The desire to find a mate is essentially no different with gay male couples than it is for other couples. Most gay men have been in a committed relationship at some point in their lives, and over half of all gay men are in some form of a relationship at any one time. However, legal same-sex marriage was not a major part of the modern gay rights movement during the past thirty years. Considering the resistance engendered by the fight for basic civil rights or for open gays in the military, legal marriage seemed unrealistic, given the political climate, and not necessarily desirable by all in the lesbian, gay, bisexual, and transgender community.

Domestic partner benefits for stable, committed gay or lesbian couples were, however, desired and pursued. Because same-sex couples weren't allowed to marry but were in stable committed relationships, and because heterosexuals who were married were given many benefits by employers and others, many lesbians and gays felt people in same-sex relationships were entitled to the same benefits.

The emphasis was on benefits that would stabilize the relationship or help one partner after the death of the other; benefits such as health insurance availability for both, pension benefits to the survivor, hospital visitation rights, bereavement leave, the right to continue living in the same apartment even if the lease was in the name of the dead partner were sought and increasingly granted in recent years. Sometimes the company or municipality granting the benefits required that the couple register as domestic partners where such registries were available.

Commitment Ceremonies

Commitment ceremonies for gay male and lesbian couples have become popular in recent years. While such ceremonies may have been occurring for thousands of years, there has been an increased focus on such ceremonies in the last few years. In one study, 19 percent of the lesbians and 11 percent of the gay men reported having a commitment ceremony. The motivation for such ceremonies varies, as we see in the example that follows.

Sam and Henry

Sam and Henry are two gay men in their early forties. Both have been in previous relationships but, until the present relationship, had never had a commitment ceremony. They did have one—which they refer to as their wedding—after having lived together for three years.

"Ritual is important to me," said Sam when questioned on his motivation for the ceremony. "I feel more married now. It was important for me to be able to stand up in front of my friends and some family members and declare to them and God that this was a holy union. The relationship has a kind of permanence that my previous relationship never had, and I think the wedding was one part of that. I always liked ritual since I was a kid. I loved being an altar boy and felt cheated out of a wedding because I was gay. Having a wedding made me feel good."

"I especially like the rings we wear" was Henry's first comment on the subject. "The ritual was important to me too, but what was even more important was having a wedding where my family could attend. My parents and my sisters and their husbands never treated my previous lover like he was my husband. They do treat Sam that way. Some of the reason, I believe, has to do with the fact that we had a wedding, and they were there. But some of the reason they accept us as married, I believe, is that we really feel married."

"Being Catholic has always been an added complication for me," Sam added. "While I reject the Church's notions on homosexuality, it still has an emotional impact on me. Having had a wedding, with the ceremony performed by an ex-seminarian, helped me to feel better. It may be irrational, but I liked it."

Sam and Henry refer to each other as husbands. They feel the ceremony helped to normalize their relationship and consider themselves to be married in all but a legal sense. Henry quipped, "We've joked about taking the first plane to Hawaii—if it becomes legal there—but would probably wait and be married in Hawaii while on a vacation. Besides, Hawaii is a lovely place for a honeymoon."

Because they are out of the mainstream, the commitment ceremonies, both religious and secular, that gays are having are extremely varied in form. Some mirror traditional marriage ceremonies; others are quite creative, incorporating a *queer* sensibility. (*Queer* is a term that encompasses the definitions of gay, lesbian, and bisexual and that has been claimed by many gay people after years of its being used as a pejorative term.) For some, the ceremony is a way to announce to the world that the relationship exists; for others, the commitment ceremony is a celebration of the relationship, a validation of the relationship, and, for many, a consecration that fulfills spiritual and religious needs. And for some, the commitment ceremony fulfills a family obligation to be married. Legal same-sex marriage would have the same effect.

Domestic Partners

It is now possible in some cities and counties for two people to register as domestic partners. While this gives the couple some of the rights and responsibilities of married couples, it also carries a strong emotional impact. In addition to providing registration papers to be filled out, San Francisco now permits a ceremony to be conducted by a city employee in conjunction with the registry. In 1996, Mayor Willie Brown and Supervisor Carole Midgen of San Francisco presided over a mass domestic partners ceremony, where hundreds of gay men and lesbians "married" each other in a joyous celebration.

If the purpose of declaring domestic partnership was only for the legal benefits that go along with the registry, then no public ceremony would have been needed. But many gays and lesbians have a need for a public declaration of their love and commitment as well as a need to normalize their lives. With television cameras recording the moment and broadcasting the event on the national evening news, this mass ceremony may have helped to heal some of the damage society at large inflicts on gays and lesbians.

The Hawaiian courts have irrevocably changed the emotional climate surrounding same-sex marriage and perhaps have also changed the priorities of the "gay agenda." Larry Kramer, the long-time gay activist and playwright and the founder of the activist group ACT UP now says the right to marry is one of the top three priorities in the queer community. The decisions by the courts in Hawaii struck a deep chord and awakened many queer people to the possibility of legal recognition of their relationships.

THE MEANINGS OF MARRIAGE

In the larger society marriage has many meanings. Culturally, it is the ultimate rite of passage. More than any other event, getting married and being married defines one as a responsible adult (having children adds to the sense of responsibility but is not essential). In the Neil Simon play and movie *Come Blow Your Horn*, the adult son is wealthy and successful in business; he dates many beautiful women and is the model of an independent adult. His parents, however, continue to call him a bum until he finally tells them he has married and is then redeemed in their eyes. He is no longer an irresponsible, childlike postadolescent, only interested in his own pleasures, but a mature, responsible adult fulfilling his obligation to his family and the community by settling down and marrying. We are raised with the notion that marriage is part of the "good life."

Marriage and Adulthood

Nothing else in our culture marks maturation the way marriage does. Other forms of marking the transition to adulthood—such as confirmation, bar mitzvah, high school graduation, college, or military service—no longer convey adult status. Confirmation and bar mitzvah are now meaningless as rites of passage—while at one time they signified the change from childhood to adulthood, today a child goes back to being the same child the day after the ceremony is over. Serving in the military and risking one's life does not convey adult status. Young army recruits are restricted from "adult" activities, such as being allowed to purchase or drink alcohol.

There is a strong negative connotation to being an adult and not being married. Unmarried men are often "bums" or considered to be playboys. Unmarried men are pictured as selfish, interested only in themselves and their own pleasures, not being responsible members of the society. Many doors are closed to singles in the corporate world. This premise was the basis of a 1995 television sitcom *Ned and Stacey*, where Ned, an advertising executive, realized his rise on the corporate ladder was stalled by his single status and so married Stacey only to get a promotion. Unmarried women are similarly seen in a negative light. They are often called "spinsters" and portrayed as needing sympathy, connoting something is essentially wrong with them. Women who are not married are often considered the child of their parents while their parents are still alive.

Legally, marriage has a special meaning. While it takes being eighteen years old to be considered a legal adult, being legally married in many states frees a person, even if she or he is under the age of eighteen, from parents' legal control.

Marriage and Self-Worth

Marriage not only has a cultural context; it is also has a highly significant personal meaning. To an individual, marriage is the ultimate validation of self-worth: "Someone wants me." This often gives the individual a sense of accomplishment; he or she has completed the rite of passage. Marriage has been presented as the "goal" of growing up; we in this culture are indoctrinated to believe we should marry eventually. This goal has been impossible for gays and lesbians to fulfill, unless they marry someone of the opposite sex; but legal same-sex marriage would make legitimate marriage possible.

Marriage is more than validation of self-worth. The commitment of marriage gives a person a sense of stability in his or her life. On a deep psychological level, it is for many men an act of submission, and from such an act comes rewards: a sense of belonging not only to the other person but to the extended family and the society that associates many rules, consequences, and rewards to the act of marriage. By marrying, a man indicates he is willing to bind himself to outside rules and accept the consequences of community property, alimony, or other responsibilities. In return, he earns the respect of others and gains inclusion into the adult community, often giving the man a sense of peace and belonging.

Marriage and Sex

Legal marriage also has another special personal meaning: it validates us as sexual people. In our sex-phobic society, all expressions of sexuality outside of marriage are officially disapproved. While for women this standard is virtually absolute, for men there is a double standard in that premarital sex is often encouraged or expected for men. Being legally married, however, frees an individual from almost all constrictions in this area. As long as the sex is within marriage, it is considered acceptable, healthy, and welcomed.

Gays and lesbians never receive such validation of their sexuality. It is never acceptable for gays or lesbians to engage in consensual adult sexual activity, whether it is promiscuous, anonymous sexual activity or sexual activity within the context of a stable, loving, committed relationship. In addition, sex between people of the same sex is still illegal in almost twenty states. The law demands, in essence, that gay men and lesbians live celibate lives. Legal same-sex marriage could change this and acknowledge that the sexual feelings and needs of gays and lesbians are valid.

Marriage and Spirituality

Marriage has spiritual meanings, as described more fully in Chapter Eight. A Jewish wedding is called a *kiddushin*, which means "to make holy." The "holy union of matrimony" is a term we have all heard many times. Protestant ministers and Jewish rabbis are expected to refrain from sex unless they are married. Marriage is virtually an expectation in most Western religions. In the Christian and Jewish religions, marriage is necessary to fulfill the commandment to "be fruitful and multiply," since having children outside of marriage is not encouraged.

Interestingly, many mainline Protestant and Jewish denominations have begun to ordain gay men and lesbians as ministers and rabbis but are struggling with how, if at all, these ministers can be sexual beings, since these religions believe sexuality is reserved for marriage, and gays and lesbians are not legally permitted to marry. Legal same-sex marriage might help also to resolve this problem.

THE IMPACT ON GAY MEN OF LEGALIZING SAME-SEX MARRIAGE

With the awareness that gay men form emotionally close and more flexible relationships than do heterosexuals, that those relationships often have different standards regarding sexuality, and that gay couples exist in a world that largely rejects them, we can begin to speculate on the emotional impact of legal same-sex marriage. We factor in the almost universal need to mate and the meaning marriage has in our society both as a rite of passage and as validation of the individual, to speculate on the possible impacts of legal same-sex marriage on gay male couples and the families they create.

Legal same-sex marriage will likely be a mixed blessing, having consequences, both positive and negative, for the couples and the individuals involved. Some of these consequences can be foreseen; others await the passage of time, should legal same-sex marriage become á reality. The impacts of legal same-sex marriage to the individual, the couple as a unit, the extended families of lesbians and gays, and the society as a whole are many. While the legal advantages are explored in Chapters Three and Seven, emotional and other impacts will be considered here.

Stabilization of Relationships

Legal marriage will probably have either a stabilizing or a destabilizing effect on different gay couples. Marriage appears to be a stabilizing force in most relationships. In the Blumstein and Schwartz study of gay, lesbian, cohabitating heterosexual, and married couples over an eighteen-month period, the gay, lesbian, and cohabitating heterosexual couples had nearly equally high rates of separation. Married couples, however, had a much lower rate of separation. While other factors (such as younger ages of the gays and lesbians) might have influenced the results, marriage appears to keep people together. For those gay male couples who desire to marry legally, the ceremony itself, the legal contract, the rings, the rituals, and the wedding photo album all enable the couple to be like a tree that is firmly rooted and yet can grow and slowly add new branches and leaves each year.

It could stabilize couples in other ways. Because marriage is a legal contract and would need to be dissolved legally, the process of dissolving the relationship would take longer than it does now. Couples that might otherwise split might find opportunities to work out their differences. Some might reconsider the consequences, especially if the idea to split was impulsive. For heterosexuals, the more barriers there are to separating, the more likely it is that a couple will stay together.

Legal marriage also could stabilize and strengthen the extended families of gays. Rejection of gays as individuals and couples by their families is not uncommon. Because gays cannot bring their partners to family functions or even possibly sleep in the same bed in the homes of other family members because they are not "married," legal marriage could defuse this situation and normalize these relationships within the context of the extended family. The sanctioning of these relationships by the state might be enough to permit some family members to put aside their prejudices and allow full participation by the gay couples in family functions. It could also help the gay man to feel he has taken his rightful place in the adult extended family as a married person and make him less likely to exclude himself from family gatherings.

Stable gay male couples would be a benefit to all of society. Since gays will continue to exist, it is in the interest of the society that they form stable couple relationships for many of the same reasons as do heterosexuals, whether or not there are children involved.

Some people suggest that homosexuals are a threat to the family and society, but there is no evidence to support this fear. The loving, caring, and supportive relationships of gays are not a threat but an asset to families and the community. It will probably be easier to integrate legally married, stable, gay couples into the community than to have them remain hidden and their relationships unsanctioned. Since many gay couples may choose to not raise children of their own, they could take a more active role in the supervision of other people's children or be foster and adoptive parents. Legally married same-sex couples could even be role models for gay teenagers, who historically have had no models of being gay, let alone being in a successful relationship.

Marriage and Couples Dealing with AIDS

AIDS is causing the death every year of thousands of gay men, many of whom are living with long-time companions. Legal same-sex marriage could also benefit many of those couples. Hospitals could no longer automatically deny visitation to the unmarried partner because he was not a member of the immediate family. Physicians would be required to consult with the husband of a gay man who is in a coma because of AIDS. The family or landlord could not automatically evict the partner from the living quarters they shared after the death of someone from AIDS.

In addition, certain inheritance rights would be guaranteed by the state. The legally married spouse would be entitled to any survivor pension benefits or bereavement leave. Lastly, it would help the widower in the grieving process. People would probably be more quick to recognize the loss of a husband than the loss of a domestic partner. The widower would probably be treated more seriously and considerately than is common now without legal same-sex marriage. All this is likely to be quite comforting to the widower in a time of great loss.

Jacque and Noel

Jacque and Noel are perhaps typical of a gay couple who desire legal marriage and would avail themselves of the option if it were available. Both are now in their early fifties, have been together for ten years, celebrated their relationship in a commitment ceremony nine years ago, and registered as domestic partners when that became available in San Francisco in 1990. Their model of a relationship is egalitarian and also happens to be monogamous. Both were previously in open relationships, but when they met each other in their early forties, both wanted something different. Each felt they wanted a relationship that was closer and possibly more stable then they had had before.

According to Noel, "Legal marriage seems like the logical next step. I just like the idea. I think it would make us feel closer, not that we need that but we want it. We own a house together, we are almost never apart. We love each other. We sleep together. We do so many things together. We are married in our own minds. This would put the imprimatur of the state on our relationship."

"I want to make a statement to the world about us," was Jacque's first comment on the subject. "This is a terribly homophobic society. I've always been a gay activist. It would make me feel wonderful to have many powerful institutions in this country be forced to deal with us as a gay couple. It would make me feel good. I think I would go out of my way to make the point whenever I could that Noel was my husband."

Both Jacque and Noel agree that legal marriage is not essential but would be nice. "We're going to go on regardless of whether we can marry or not," Noel adds. "Legally we've taken care of everything we can. It's not going to make a big difference to us in that regard. Where it will matter is emotionally. And that's important to me."

LEGAL MARRIAGES AND DESTABILIZATION

Legal marriage also has the possibility of destabilizing relationships that have been stable for a long time. If it were available, some couples who were doing fine without legal marriage might avail themselves of the option if one of them wanted it more than the other. Coercion around marriage is usually a prescription for failure. The result may be that some of the couples will split up—something that might not have happened if they were never legally married. There is a high divorce rate among stable cohabitating heterosexuals couples who eventually marry. Couples often get into trouble when one of the partners is forced into a situation he or she does not want to be in.

Lacking the opportunity to marry legally, gay men have been quite creative in establishing alternative mating arrangements. Many of these relationships specifically fit the personality and nature of gay men (closeness, flexibility, and open sexuality). Some of these arrangements have been truly creative. This would always still be an option. Marriage, however, is a powerful and a conservative institution with history, tradition, and rules. There would undoubtedly be pressure on gay male couples to conform to the traditional model of heterosexual relationships, both to be married and to imitate heterosexual marriage.

Arthur

Arthur is an angry queer activist. He has been fighting for civil rights for gay people for over twenty years. For most of the last year he has been telling all who would listen what a disaster he believes legal same-sex marriage would be for gays. "Marriage is a bankrupt institution. It doesn't work for straights, and it won't work for us. We've been doing just fine without it. If I were dating a guy who wanted to legally marry, I would show him the door. I want a man who doesn't need the government to tell him our relationship is okay." Arthur's feelings are shared by a number of others in the gay male community.

Just as legal marriage would affect gay couples, it would also have a profound impact on gay individuals. For many gay men, the impact will be positive. Our society is cruel to those who grow up lesbian or gay. Society tells gay men that they are wrong, that they are sick mentally (until 1973, psychiatry officially pathologized homosexuality), that they are criminal in their behavior (consensual adult homosexual activity is still against the law in nearly twenty states), or that they are spiritually sinful and immoral. The result may be a damaged individual who often believes some of these things he has been told. For many gay men, mating outside of legal marriage has been one avenue to healing and growth.

Simply having the option of legal same-sex marriage available, whether or not the individual avails himself of it, will have a positive impact on the self-image of many gay men. For many gay men, having grown up with the internal conflict over whether there was something wrong with him, being able now to marry legally and have that validated by the state may be both normalizing and reparative. For some older gay men, such validation might be taken as an apology for past torment; for younger gay men, it may be seen as a statement by the state that they are normal, both for wanting to mate with men and for wanting to have close personal relationships.

In an informal survey I conducted among gay men in San Francisco asking if they would avail themselves of legal same-sex marriage, those who have answered in the affirmative have mostly cited (in addition to the legal benefits) how they imagine they would feel if they were allowed to marry someone of the same sex. The response I heard most when asking gay people why they would consider legal same-sex marriage is that they believe "it will feel good." When further questioned, respondents essentially say legal marriage would be a validation of their relationships by the state, or, as one gay man put it, it would be the "ultimate legitimization before all of society." For a few, it would also mean fitting in better with their extended family.

But all the benefits for individuals may not be positive. For some gay men, the rewards of inclusion into adult society that might come with legal same-sex marriage—whether monetary, career, familial, or psychological—might not seem worth the price. Marriage might be seen as another pressure, one they thought they had escaped by being gay. If legal same-sex marriage is available, there will undoubtedly be more pressure on gay men to mate and marry, and not all will welcome that pressure. One might imagine a situation sometime in the future in which an openly gay man might feel pressure to find a man to marry in order to get a career promotion or to not be disinherited by the family.

Another potential disadvantage of same-sex legal marriage for gay men might be the entire matter of legal divorce. All the problems now associated with legal heterosexual divorce would be a possibility in gay relationships: the lawyers, the mediators, the expenses, the loss of privacy. Without legal same-sex marriage, these legal problems are minimized. Legal same-sex marriage would involve the state in what many consider to be essentially a private matter. For some who are arguing for getting the state out of the marriage business entirely (with the understanding there would still be a need to ensure parental responsibilities to children) and letting churches have the final word on blessing and sanctifying couples, legal same-sex marriage seems like a step backward. There are probably any number of divorced men who wish they were never allowed to legally say "I do."

SAME-SEX MARRIAGE AND GAY FAMILIES

If there is one area where legal same-sex marriage will most likely have a positive impact, it is in the area of families that gays and lesbians are creating. Lesbians and gays, in unprecedented numbers, are raising children. One newsletter for gay couples, edited by Bryant and Demian, reported that one in ten gay men are "caring" for children, whether in their custody or not. In the same report, 4 percent of the men and 10 percent of the women said they planned to have children.

Gay Parents

While some lesbians and gays have always raised children from former heterosexual marriages or liaisons, many lesbians and gays are now intentionally choosing to become parents and raise children as single parents or as part of same-sex couples. Newspapers serving the lesbian and gay community in many cities in the country now list resources for lesbians and gays who are parents or who want to become parents. A search on the World Wide Web finds dozens of sites where one can find information about gay families.

Congregation Sha'ar Zahav, a Jewish synagogue in San Francisco with a special outreach to lesbians and gays, now has 500 adult members and 150 children in the congregation. In the early 1980s, there were almost no children in the congregation. Today the congregation has a fully functioning Hebrew school for the children. Similar examples are seen in other cities and other denominations.

There has always been a desire on the part of gay people to raise children, but for a long time this option was denied to them. Even recently, as Chapter Three describes, lesbians and gays are continuing to lose their own biological children in custody disputes to their former partners simply because of their sexual orientation.

Despite such legal issues, a "gayby boom" is now in progress. Gay men are adopting, becoming foster care parents, paying surrogates to have their children, impregnating lesbians and creating alternative families, or raising the children from their previous heterosexual marriages and relationships. Such parenting will continue regardless of the outcome of the movement for legal same-sex marriage. If the government is truly interested in supporting the family—all families— then it should seriously consider making legal same-sex marriage available in all states.

Children of Gay Parents

Children in families headed by lesbian or gay individuals or couples do not suffer because of that fact. Suffering was an argument made by the State of Hawaii but refuted by the plaintiffs in *Baehr* v. *Miike*. Many studies have shown that the children of lesbian and gay families fare as well as the children of heterosexual families. It is difficult being a child, even when the child has loving parents who can give him or her most of what he or she needs. Children are continually changing and growing, physically, mentally and emotionally. They have a need for stability around them in order to deal with the changes that are happening to them.

As Chapter Three describes, the stability that would be provided by the legal protections—ability for the nonbiological parent to adopt, inheritance rights, visitation rights should the parents separate—would all be emotionally comforting to the child. Simply knowing that life would go on if one of the parents died would be a small measure of comfort. Some gay couples have used the homophobic laws as they now exist to exclude a nonbiological parent from visitation after a break up, even when there was a written contract agreeing to such visitations. Legal same-sex marriage would stop this. The children would be further protected and would benefit.

Children also like to fit in with their peers. Just as it would be more comforting for a child if the heterosexual parents were married rather than merely cohabitating with their partner, the child in a gay family would also be comforted. It would also allow the parents to demonstrate commitment in relationships to the child, regardless of whether the child turns out to be homosexual or heterosexual.

Tommy and Nicholas

Tommy and Nicholas, two gay men, have adopted and are raising two children. The mother of one of the children was addicted to crack when the child was born, and the other child has other special needs. Because they live in and adopted the children in a progressive county in California, they were able to adopt the children jointly. Both are the legal parents of both of the children.

When asked if they would marry if it were available, Tommy replied in the affirmative. "I would like to get married. I think I would like it for Nicholas and myself. But it would also help the children. Right now the kids are young and don't really understand anything about marriage. But I think when they get older, maybe when they become teenagers, I think it would make it a little easier for them if they could say their parents are married. It would make them a little more like the other kids. They have enough other things to deal with."

Nicholas chimed in, "It would make it easier for us, especially in dealing with teachers and child-care workers. We wouldn't have to explain it all the time. Right now it's not too hard because they are both in private preschool, and we know their teachers were told specifically what the situation was with us. But there have already been other situations where we had to go through a long explanation of our relationship and our relationship to the boys. It would be easier if we were a married couple and could just say that we adopted the boys. That would make it easier for us and easier for them."

CONCLUSION

In summary, gay couples and gay families are functioning quite nicely without legal same-sex marriage. The option to marry, however, would add another dimension that would likely stabilize and normalize many gay male relationships and families headed by gay male couples. In other situations, it might actually destabilize a relationship that would otherwise be stable. It will probably be a mixed blessing. The impact will only clearly be seen after it becomes a reality, should that happen. Most people in the gay community would welcome having the option so that they could decide for themselves if they wished to avail themselves of legal same-sex marriage.

References

Bailey, J. M., & Zucker, K. J. (1995). Childhood sex-typed behaviors and sexual orientation: A conceptual analysis and quantitative review. *Developmental Psychology, 31*, 43–55.

Bell, A. P., & Weinberg, M. S. (1978). *Homosexualities: A study of diversity among men and women.* New York: Simon and Schuster.

Bell, A. P., Weinberg, M. S., & Hammersmith, S. K. (1981). *Sexual preference: Its development in men and women.* Bloomington: Indiana University Press.

Bettinger, M. (1986). *Relationship satisfaction, cohesion and adaptability: A study of gay male couples.* Unpublished doctoral dissertation, California Graduate School of Marital and Family Therapy, San Rafael, CA.

Blumstein, P. & Schwartz, P. (1983). *American couples: Money, work and sex.* New York: Morrow.

Boswell, J. (1995). *Same-sex unions in premodern Europe.* New York: Vintage Books.

Bryant, S., & Demian, B. (Eds.). (1990, May/June). *Partners: Newsletter for gay and lesbian couples.* (Available from Partners, Box 9685, Seattle, WA 98109.)

Carter, E., & McGoldrick, M. (Eds.). (1980). *The family life cycle: A framework for therapy.* New York: Gardner Press.

Chauncey, G. (1994). *Gay New York: Gender, urban culture and the making of the gay male world, 1890–1940.* New York: Basic Books.

Freedman, J. (1878). *Happy people.* New York: Harcourt Brace Jovanovich.

Green, R.-J., Bettinger, M., & Zacks, E. (1996). Are lesbian couples fused and gay male couples disengaged? In J. Laird & R.-J. Green (Eds.), *Lesbians and gays in couples and families: A handbook for therapists* (pp. 185–230). San Francisco: Jossey-Bass.

Harry, J. (1982). Decision making and age differences among gay male couples. *Journal of Homosexuality, 8*(2), 9–21.

Harry, J. (1984). *Gay couples.* New York: Praeger.

Harry, J., & DuVall, W. B. (1978). *The social organization of gay males.* New York: Praeger.

Herek, G. M. (1994). Assessing heterosexuals' attitudes toward lesbian and gay men: A review of empirical research with the ATLG Scale. In B. Greene & G. M. Herek (Eds.), *Lesbian and gay psychology: Theory, research and clinical applications* (pp. 206–228). Thousand Oaks, CA: Sage.

Karlen, A. (1971). *Sexuality and homosexuality: A new view.* New York: Norton.

Katz, J. N. (1990, January–March). "The invention of heterosexuality." *Socialist Review, 20,* 7–34.

Kurdek, L. A., (1991). Correlates of relationship satisfaction in cohabitating gay and lesbian couples: Integration of contextual, investment and problem solving models. *Journal of Personality and Social Psychology, 61,* 910–922.

Kurdek, L. A., (1991). The dissolution of gay and lesbian couples. *Journal of Social and Personal Relationships, 8,* 265–278.

Kurdek, L. A., (1993). The allocation of household labor in homosexual and heterosexual cohabitating couples. *Journal of Social Issues, 49,* 27–139.

Kurdek, L. A., & Schmitt, J. P. (1986). Relationship quality of partners in heterosexual married, heterosexual cohabitating and gay and lesbian relationships. *Journal of Personality and Social Psychology, 51,* 711–720.

Kurdek, L. A., & Schmitt, J. P. (1987). Partner monogamy in married, heterosexual cohabitating, gay and lesbian couples. *Journal of Sex Research, 23,* 212–232.

Levinger, G. (1979). A social psychological perspective on marital dissolution. In G. Levinger & O. C. Moles (Eds.), *Divorce and separation* (pp. 37–63). New York: Basic Books.

Martin, T. C., & Bumpass, L. L. (1989). Recent trends in marital disruption. *Demography, 6*, 37.

McWhirter, D. P., & Mattison, A. M. (1984). *The male couple: How relationships develop*. Englewood Cliffs, NJ: Prentice-Hall.

Morin, S. F. (1977). Heterosexual bias in psychological research on lesbianism and male homosexuality. *American Psychologist, 32*, 629–637.

Peplau, L. A. (1981). What homosexuals want in relationships. *Psychology Today, 15*(3) 28–40.

Peplau, L. A. (1991). Lesbian and gay relationships. In J. C. Gonsiorek & J. D. Weinrich (Eds.), *Homosexuality: Research implications for public policy* (pp. 177–196). Newbury Park, CA: Sage.

Peplau, L. A., & Cochran, S. D. (1980, September). *Sex differences in values concerning love relationships*. Paper presented at the annual meeting of the American Psychological Association, Montreal, Canada.

Shernoff, M. (1995). Male couples and their relationships styles. *Journal of Gay and Lesbian Social Services, 2*(2).

Silverstein, C. (1981). *Man to man: Gay couples in America*. New York: Morrow.

Thompson, L., & Walker, A. J. (1989). Women and men in marriage, work and parenthood. *Journal of Marriage and the Family, 53*, 928–940.

Tripp, C. (1975). *The homosexual matrix*. New York: McGraw Hill.

Zacks, E., Green, R.-J., & Marrow, J. (1988). Comparing lesbian and heterosexual couples on the circumplex model: An initial investigation. *Family Process, 27*, 471–484.

5

Mental Health Issues and Same-Sex Marriage

MARK TOWNSEND

As part of the journey toward same-sex marriage, looking ahead to the future will be important. This chapter outlines some of the broad psychological and emotional issues that all same-sex relationships currently face and speculates on the effect that legally sanctioned same-sex relationships might have on couples in the future. Though not necessarily predictive of where we will go, an understanding of both the obstacles and the attractions ahead helps ensure our journey's success.

A chapter devoted to the mental health issues surrounding same-sex marriage must first make the case for the inclusion of such issues within the same-sex marriage debate. The idea that the prevention of such marriages has specific and negative mental health implications may strike some as unexpected, at worst, and unfounded, at best. Many mental health professionals believe that, by strengthening the legal context of same-sex relationships, one also strengthens the emotional stability of lesbian and gay couples. The mainstream press also has picked up on this idea.

Hard data for this argument is difficult to come by, however, since there is much current evidence of emotional stability in lesbian and gay couples and in the children they rear, as I will explain in this chapter. Until cohorts of legally married gay couples exist with which to compare with non–legally married couples, we must be cautious in attributing the difficulties experienced by some gay couples to their inability to be legally wed.

The question of whether marriage would lead to emotionally healthier gay couples is a complicated one. The arguments put forth in this chapter take into account the varying reports about the health status of gay men and lesbians. An intangible factor that underlies many of the following points is the role played by society's aversion to homosexuality—namely, homophobia. The extent to which lesbians and gay men internalize this homophobia and, as a result, think of their sexuality as something shameful is almost certainly a larger factor in their mental health than their inability to marry. Yet societal homophobia is the main force preventing gay marriage. Which will change first: heterosexism or the construct of marriage? This chapter will describe whether legal recognition of gay marriage may result in a lessening of homophobia and therefore improve the mental health of all gay people, coupled or not.

THE MENTAL HEALTH OF LESBIAN AND GAY COUPLES

To attempt to understand the effects of marriage and the denial of marriage on gay and lesbian couples, we can first briefly review what is known about such couples. It appears that, at least among gay men, the heterosexual married model of two people cohabiting, although quite common, is a less frequent occurrence than among heterosexuals. As David McWhirter and Drew Mattison describe, gay men may think of themselves as a couple yet might live in different houses, or even different continents. They may make a joint decision not to be monogamous. In addition, one partner in such a couple may be legally married to and happily living with a female spouse.

Male Couples

The mental health issues surrounding male couples have been described using a number of constructs. In general, however, information about the mental health of gay male couples has been drawn from clinical observations. McWhirter and Mattison developed a stage model, in which problems emerge for male couples either in the context of specific stages or when individuals in a couple progressed through the stages at different rates (see Chapter One for the details of this model). For example, McWhirter and Mattison identify common problems for couples who have been together six to ten years (they must continue to develop communication skills, for example, and those who do not, risk feeling trapped with one another). Further, Mattison and McWhirter report that they find degrees of stage discrepancy in the majority of couples they see clinically: one partner may exhibit behaviors and attitudes that the other dealt with years ago.

Some of the problems experienced by coupled gay men may be the result of the socialization of men in general. Some men reportedly have difficulty in forming and maintaining intimate bonds. According to Robert Cabaj and Shelly Klinger, some male couples may have more difficulty than lesbian or heterosexual couples in establishing close ties due to a lack of the requisite nurturing social skills. A frequently noted fear of intimacy found in some gay male couples may actually be a learned reaction that gay men develop as a protective response to earlier homophobic experiences.

Lesbian Couples

Mental health issues for lesbian couples have been characterized very differently than those for gay couples. This is not surprising, given the different social roles men and women are often expected to assume. Nevertheless, evidence both from case studies and from psychological research using structured interviewing appears to support the claim that lesbian couples achieve a greater degree of mutuality than other couples, including heterosexual ones. In addition, Charlotte Patterson reports that as lesbians divide their labor more equally, their children are more likely to be well adjusted. There is not, however, universal agreement that lesbian couples are inherently more fair in their distribution of labor. Reilly and Lynch demonstrated great inequality in terms of which lesbian partner makes decisions for the couple, though their research lacked comparison groups of heterosexual or gay male couples. Further reflecting on the differences between lesbian couples and other couples, Green has criticized the use of Freudian and neo-Freudian psychological theories with lesbian couples, with their emphasis on increasing personal autonomy. She argues instead for the use of therapeutic perspectives that "envision individual development as occurring *within the context of relationships*" (italics added).

The mental health challenges of lesbian couples are frequently viewed as springing from a too-intense interdependency; in other words, couples with a greater ability to achieve "closeness," as measured in a variety of ways, can also lose their sense of individual purpose and identity. This has been described as *merging* in the clinical literature and is seen as the cause of such problems as early breakups or a decline in sexual activity. The effect of legal marriage on a lesbian couple with intense interdependency is, again, difficult to ascertain before the legalization of same-sex marriages. To paraphrase an old joke, just because you bring a moving van on the second date does not mean that you desire all the legal ramifications of marriage.

THE EFFECT OF MARRIAGE ON MENTAL HEALTH

How can the availability of legal marriage help the mental health of lesbian and gay couples? Research with heterosexuals has shown beneficial health effects (both mental and physical) of couplehood for men but not for women. Whether there will be any protective effects of coupling for lesbians and gay men is unknown.

The mental health problems just described play themselves out quite differently from couple to couple. Couples who fear intimacy may, of course, rush into legal union in the hope that this will magically change their ambivalence—just as many heterosexual couples do. It is more likely, however, that couples will choose marriage in a reasoned way during a time of nesting, to return to one of McWhirter and Mattison's stages. There is no way to know how many lesbian and gay couples experience difficulties with intimacy—whether too much or too little—and certainly many couples do not. Other important questions can be answered only after legal union is a possibility: will married lesbian and gay couples experience greater satisfaction than nonmarried ones? Will their relationships last longer? And what about the health of such relationships: will the individuals involved continue their personal growth, in a fashion similar to those who chose not to marry, yet remain coupled?

THE CHILDREN OF GAY AND LESBIAN COUPLES

No mental health problems have been identified as particular to the children of lesbians and gay men. In fact, researchers such as Charlotte Patterson report that these children are functioning at least as well as those of heterosexual couples, if not better. An ironic byproduct of this literature, acknowledged by Patterson herself, is that even gay-affirmative researchers suggest it is a good outcome if the children of lesbians and gay men develop into heterosexual adults at rates consistent with those of the general population, implying that that the alternative result would be an adverse event. Members of the lesbian and gay community argue that it is perfectly all right if their children are eventually found more likely to be gay.

To say otherwise is not only to demean themselves but to suggest to their children, some of whom will indeed be homosexual or bisexual, that being gay is shameful.

However, it is important to emphasize that studies indicate that the sexual orientation of the children is not affected by their parents being gay or lesbian (the genetic effect is still undetermined). For example, Michael Bailey found that the adult sons of gay fathers were over 90 percent heterosexual and that the sexual orientation of the sons was not affected by the amount of time spent with the gay fathers. Many of the cohorts of children of gay parents available for study are still preadolescent: it may turn out that children of gay- and lesbian-parented households are, in fact, more likely to be gay, as their emergence into adolescence and adulthood is studied; but to date, the more important point is that sexual orientation appears unlikely to be dramatically affected by parenting from gay men or lesbians.

The identified mental health issues of gay- and lesbian-parented families tend to be framed around the way these families choose to interact with the world. Gay families deal with societal homophobia in different ways, and we do not yet have sufficient information to know which is the "best" way to rear children in these families. The consensus among gay-affirmative psychotherapists such as April Martin is for parents to be open about their homosexuality, both with their children and with other adults. This makes perfect sense: if Daddy never discusses the relationship he has with his lover, much less talks to his child's teacher about anti-gay speech in the classroom, he is doing little to mitigate the effects of homophobia on that child. Worse, he is causing his child to think of his family as abnormal, leading the child to wonder if he or she is at fault. But coming out to major figures in the lives of gay parents and their children is no easy task, and the difficulty varies widely from place to place—San Francisco versus Lubbock, Texas, for example. Many gay parents develop certain ways of responding to the inevitable question, Where's your husband or wife? Lesbian and gay parents may take a personal inventory of the ways they perceive homosexuality to limit their lives, realistically or not—a self-assessment that will provide guidance regarding when, if ever, the family must be guarded about disclosing the parents' sexual orientation. Legal same-sex marriage would help legitimize the couples' interaction with the world, especially where children are concerned.

THE PSYCHOLOGICAL IMPACT OF MARRIAGE CEREMONIES

The marriage ceremony, the wedding, represents one part of an interesting duality. The agreement to enter into marriage is a private one, but the actual ceremony of commitment is, for many, very public and often involves symbols—something borrowed, something blue—that, while they may be used personally, are really props for well-known social roles. It is also often the case that heterosexual couples will have small, legal ceremonies—with the requisite witnesses and the proper authority figure to preside over it—and have a larger, celebratory event later.

In the same way that lesbian and gay couples may choose a variety of living situations, lesbian and gay commitment rites also occur in many different ways. What is missing is the patina of governmental authorization and, in many cases, the support of organized religion. While these are not small things, it is unknown whether they limit the joy experienced by those lesbians and gay men who choose a wedding ceremony or those who attend it. We must also acknowledge the debate in the lesbian and gay community about whether weddings as such are in the community's best interest, considering that marriage has historically had several meanings, including the legal transfer of "ownership" of the bride from her father to her husband.

That aside, how do lesbian and gay couples choose to declare their mutual involvement to the world? As befits cultures—the lesbian and gay one, that is—free from societal expectations, ceremonies can range from full-throttle church weddings, preacher included, to simple ceremonies that recall the illegal weddings of African American slaves, to ceremonies recalling those of pre-Christian Europe. Similarly, newly "married" couples may legally change their last names to a hyphenated hybrid or even to a new, chosen name.

Some big questions regarding the mental health advantages of wedding ceremonies remain unexplored, however, both for gay people and for heterosexuals. One must keep in mind the societal expectation for cohabiting heterosexuals to eventually become married—an expectation that brings with it its own emotional hazards. Society is only now acknowledging the existence of long-term gay couples. Should legal recognition of same-sex couples become widely available, overly intrusive parents may ask, So when are you going to marry this person?

THE PSYCHOLOGICAL EFFECTS OF ADVERSE LEGAL JUDGMENTS

This section addresses the psychological issues lesbian and gay couples and their children face following the couple's separation or the divorce of a legal marriage in which one partner is gay. (Legal issues involved are explored in Chapters Three and Seven.) The effects brought about by the lack of legal recognition of gay unions and its underlying homophobia are seen most clearly in this arena. Adverse legal judgments regarding lesbian and gay parents have had perhaps the most tragic results and are the most widely publicized.

The Sharon Bottoms case sadly demonstrates the intersection between institutional homophobia and the lack of legal union. In this widely publicized case, a lesbian mother, Sharon Bottoms, lost custody of her son to her own mother, in part because she was living with a female partner. The trial court judge ignored the evidence presented that lesbians and gay men are fit parents, and used religious rhetoric to openly disparage Bottoms's "homosexual lifestyle."

In affirming the judge's decision, the Virginia Supreme Court claimed to not be basing its decision on Bottoms's sexual orientation, but this is obviously untrue. If Ms. Bottoms and her partner had been legally married in Virginia, the court would have taken into account the general case law concerning custody of children, and it would have been extremely difficult for a grandparent to win custody from a parent. This decision certainly affected Sharon Bottoms and her son, but it also struck fear into the hearts of lesbian and gay parents throughout the United States—will I have to someday choose between my child and my same-sex spouse in order to retain custody?

This is not to say that all courts have been unfriendly to lesbians and gay men seeking custody. A recent study by Connolly described seventeen gay couples in the United States in which the nonbiological partner had been granted second-parent rights—that is, rights to parenthood that do not terminate the right of any biological parent. Successful petitioners were often portrayed as having both high economic and social status, suggesting that lower-middle-class petitioners would have a harder job convincing a court they deserved parental rights. As presented more fully in Chapter Three, seventeen states have granted second-parent adoptions.

Effects on Lesbian and Gay Parents and Their Partners

It is important also to recognize the psychological plight of the nonbiological parent. Psychologists such as Lockman disagree with the term *nonbiological* and prefer the term *nongenetic* instead, because the attachment process between infant and caregiver sets down biological roots. Similar to baby ducks, which bond biologically with their mother, human infants, given the proper nurturing and dependable environment, bond with—become attached to—those who regularly care for them. One study by McCandlish found no significant differences in the degree to which the biological and nonbiological lesbian mother was bonded to the child. Whether court-ordered or the result of a breakup, cutoffs between infants and nonbiological parents can have lasting behavioral and psychological consequences for the child. Dundas asserts that prior to any breakup, "overt and covert" mechanisms at work both within lesbian and gay relationships and the society with which they interact may ensure that the nonbiological parent is not the principal caregiver and that the child does not develop a normal attachment to her or him.

Regarding adoption itself, the picture is varied but, for the most part, discouraging. While a handful of states have allowed joint adoption by lesbian couples, in many states being openly gay or lesbian is considered presumptive of unfitness if it is discovered during the adoption process. Only two states, Florida and New Hampshire, currently forbid lesbian and gay adoptions outright. Foster parenting is similarly discouraged in many states. This is not to say that lesbians and gay men are not adopting children or providing them foster care; just that they are doing so discretely, often with the long-term partner of the adoptive/foster parent going into virtual hiding. Again, relationships are stressed and emotional bonds weakened by this homophobic system, which can thoughtlessly drive couples apart.

Effects on Children

The potential mental health problems engendered by these legal hurdles can be myriad. Children who are placed apart from their biological parents often experience varying degrees of trauma, as do their parents. As David Purcell and Daniel Hicks describe it, the trauma begins in the courtroom, as people hear their lives and their lovers distorted and demonized. Children are denied access to attachment figures while the often lengthy legal process continues, irreparably changing both the fabric of their childhood and their future relationships with parents and guardians. And it remains the case that foster children are denied access to millions of potential adoptive parents—lesbians and gay men.

Effects of Separation

The lack of legal recognition of lesbian and gay couples also has important mental health implications when couples separate. Nonbiological parents rarely have guaranteed access to children they may have reared together with their partners. In most jurisdictions, the nonbiological parent has access to his or her child at the pleasure of the biological parent, because legally they are considered "biological strangers" to that child. As might be imagined, cases abound in which angry biological parents have prevented their former partners from seeing the children they have reared together. Ironically, in some cases, homophobic arguments are used by lesbians and gay men to keep their ex-partners from having contact with nonbiological children.

But of course for most lesbians and gay men, separation concerns dividing up property, not children. Here again, there are both constraints and freedoms in the current situation. Gay couples who reside in community property states, in which 50 percent of assets are distributed between divorcing couples, are free to come up with other arrangements. Many would not consider that a freedom, however, since long-term gay partners are also free to place the possessions of the ex-partner in the street or to pay no alimony. Legal marriage would help regulate the dissolution of these unions. It might also be fair to assume that some lesbians and gay men will avoid legal marriage if only to avoid the hassle of a divorce. Legal marriage, or at least the ability to choose it, will allow couples a new and perhaps healthier viewpoint from which to consider whether to become more committed to each other.

Effects of Illness

The legal rights of couples who find themselves confronting the serious illness of one or both partners represent a mixed picture. On the negative side, few hospitals automatically grant visitation privileges, much less the authority to make major decisions, to a gay partner. The psychological trauma inflicted upon excluded surviving lesbian and gay spouses by having their partners die in the company of their family of origin, who have made treatment decisions without consulting or even knowing about the surviving partners, is profound. Fortunately, in the United States, two people are free to declare that one will make decisions for the other in the event that he or she becomes incapacitated—to appoint a durable power of attorney for health care—and can prevent the nightmare just mentioned. Even with this protection, however, some gay men and lesbians have been denied the right to make such decisions in emergency situations because they did not have the necessary documentation with them.

Another tragedy, also preventable, occurs when one partner dies without executing a will. Many middle-aged lesbians and gay men have not yet composed one, much less thought through the aftermath of an untimely death. Without a will, surviving partners have their grief compounded by the fact that the partner's living biological heirs, and not the survivor, may inherit, say, half the house and the entire contents of the deceased's life savings. In addition, few if any pension plans provide for a surviving gay spouse.

PSYCHOLOGICAL EFFECTS
OF THE LACK OF LEGAL UNIONS

What relation, if any, does the lack of legal union have to any of the mental health problems noted in the lesbian and gay community? This question is difficult to answer, because too little research has been performed to determine whether the prevalence of mental illness is any different from that in the heterosexual community, and because no comparison groups of married gay couples yet exist. Here, as well, the task is to think through the following: would legal marriage in some way enhance the psychological health among lesbians and gay men?

Homophobia

The role of negative life events in the development of psychiatric conditions, whether it be major depression or borderline personality disorder, is well known. The extent to which society's subtle and not-so-subtle anti-gay bias—representing a long series of negative life events for gay individuals—affects the rates of psychiatric disorders among gay men and lesbians is nearly impossible to determine. One would have to find a comparison group of gay people living completely free of such bias from their earliest childhood in order to say with any certainty that homophobia causes mental illness.

Many gay-affirmative health care workers have argued that the special burden homophobia places on gay people increases the rates of certain conditions, although this has not been demonstrated convincingly. Other gay-affirmative researchers have avoided examining the issue of psychiatric illnesses among gay people because of psychiatry's past. Mental health trainees have, until recently, been taught using psychoanalytic case studies emphasizing that lesbians and gay men suffer from mental illness at higher rates than heterosexuals, because the *disorder* of homosexuality (as it was once considered) was the common result of faulty parenting.

Suicide and Young Lesbians and Gay Men

Given the viewpoints just described, it is valid to discuss individual mental health problems found in the lesbian and gay community and consider how legal marriage might reduce their impact. Why do lesbian and gay youths appear to be attempting suicide at higher rates, and how would societal approval of their sexual orientation in the form of legal gay marriages affect this? The study of gay youth suicide is itself controversial for a variety of reasons: some researchers are reluctant to label children and adolescents as gay too early in their lives; some researchers have tried to identify, postmortem, the sexuality of those who commit suicide.

Many reports, although of varying methodological rigor, have demonstrated greater suicidal behavior among lesbian and gay youth between the ages sixteen to twenty-four than among heterosexual youth. While many risk factors have been identified, ranging from the presence of mental illness—surely a logical cause—to an unsupportive family environment, other less tangible causes are certainly at play. If gay and lesbian adolescents were able, openly, to have crushes, to date, and to declare their love for one another, with the expectation that one day such love might lead to marriage—just as for heterosexual adolescents—an immediate benefit would surely be an increase in self-esteem. Such a reduction in societal homophobia will be accomplished in small increments, however, and does little to protect the gay youth whose parents believe it is important to teach them that their "lifestyle choice" is wrong and throw them out of the house.

Substance Abuse

Although there is not complete agreement, there is some indication that lesbians and gay men have more substance abuse problems than heterosexuals. How legal marriage might affect substance abuse treatment for lesbians and gay men is debatable. As Robert Cabaj describes, services such as married couples' group therapy or concurrent AA and Al-Anon groups often overtly or covertly exclude gay couples. And there is evidence that lesbians and gay men have special needs while in recovery. For example, Vicky Mays interviewed African American lesbians in treatment centers and found fewer social supports than existed for African American heterosexual alcoholics. Another study by Hall documented other perceived barriers to recovery by lesbians, including barriers erected by the present health care system itself.

Although no guarantee against discrimination, legal marriage for same-sex couples might spur some gay couples to accept nothing less than full integration, if not equivalent services. Whether gay people do better in recovery in gay-only settings, or in settings that are gay-affirmative but include heterosexual clients, is a matter of current debate. Cabaj also points out that couples whose social lives revolve around a bar scene may have an especially difficult time establishing clean and sober friends, if few other social outlets exist in their communities. One can only wonder what new and self-affirming social structures might emerge for legally married gay and lesbian couples to aid in their sobriety.

Domestic Violence

The arrival of legal same-sex marriage should lend gay and lesbian relationships a higher profile, with possible multiple benefits in other mental health arenas. For instance, same-sex domestic violence is only now receiving greater attention, perhaps for the same reason that earlier gay-affirmative health care writers avoided discussing other mental health issues: the information could be misused. There is no evidence that domestic violence occurs more frequently among lesbians and gay men, but it does occur, and fewer resources are available to help these couples. Although it is unlikely that legalizing same-sex marriages would reduce domestic violence, considering that the rates of such violence in the heterosexual and homosexual communities are probably equivalent, same-sex domestic violence might be taken more seriously by police authorities after marriages are legalized, and shelters and other services might become more gay-sensitive.

CONCLUSION

Imagine two different United States sometime in the next century: one with the legal recognition of same-sex couples and one without. From this vantage point, the mental health implications of the presence or absence of same-sex marriage are not entirely clear. In both places, marriage ceremonies between people of the same sex have become increasingly common. More children are being reared by gay and lesbian couples than ever before. Current issues in the health care of gay men and lesbians, from AIDS to breast cancer to substance abuse, have been clarified and perhaps resolved.

But something is amiss in the United States that actively chose to deny lesbians and gay men the ability to marry legally. The civil rights of gay citizens have only marginally improved, and most gay Americans live, by necessity, in the closet. Outside of a few cities, homosexuality is not presented as a normal way of living, either in the schools or in the media. And the debate over gays in the military has been resolved: there are none permitted.

In the other United States, the one that allowed and accepted same-sex marriage, we find another nation entirely. Fewer gay men and lesbians live in "gay ghettos." No mental health professional refers to the trauma that gay people experience when they have children and live among heterosexuals, because fewer people think of the communities as that separate. Hate speech occurs, of course, but it is labeled as such. Anti-gay humor and icons are relegated to the trash pile, except among certain gay people who collect them for their historical value. And all Americans, starting in elementary school, are taught that gay people are to be included in the legal rights to housing and employment.

At this point, it is unclear which United States will be the future. This much is certain, though: change is difficult to accept, both for individuals and for society as a whole. And we are now in a time of great potential change. The fate of same-sex marriage rests entirely on the fate of homophobia. As we continue our individual comings out, to the new neighbor or to our physician; as we act to counter negative depictions of gay people in the schoolyard and in the media; as we work to promote full equality among people, regardless of sexual orientation or adherence to "normal" gender roles, we ease the way for same-sex legal union. As we influence the heterosexual majority in these ways we also make ourselves stronger, and this growing emotional strength may be the lasting mental health legacy of the current fight for same-sex marriage.

References

Blumfield, K. (1993). A comparison of alcohol consumption between lesbians and heterosexual women in an urban population. *Drug and Alcohol Dependence, 33,* 257–269.

Bux, D. A. (1996). The epidemiology of problem drinking in gay men and lesbians: A critical review. *Clinical Psychology Review, 16,* 277–298.

Cabaj, R. P. (1996). Substance abuse in gay men, lesbians, and bisexuals. In R. P. Cabaj & T. S. Stein (Eds.), *Textbook of homosexuality and mental health.* Washington, DC: American Psychiatric Press.

Cabaj, R .P., & Klinger, R. L. (1996). Psychotherapeutic interventions with lesbians and gay men. In R. P. Cabaj & T. S. Stein (Eds.), *Textbook of homosexuality and mental health.* Washington, DC: American Psychiatric Press.

Connolly, C. (1996). The description of gay and lesbian families in judicial opinions in same-sex second-parent adoption cases. Association paper, The Society for the Study of Social Problems, Washington, DC.

Curry, H., Clifford, D., & Leonard, R. (1993). Looking ahead: Estate planning. In H. Curry, D. Clifford, & R. Leonard (Eds.), *A legal guide for lesbian and gay couples.* Berkeley: Nolo Press.

Dundas, S. (forthcoming). Family therapy in gay and lesbian parented families. *Journal of the Gay and Lesbian Medical Association.*

Let them wed. (1996, January 6). *The Economist,* 13–14.

Ettelbrick, P. L. (1992). Since when is marriage a path to liberation? In S. Sherman (Ed.), *Lesbian and gay marriage: Private commitments, public ceremonies.* Philadelphia: Temple University Press.

Gibson, P. (1989). Gay male and lesbian youth suicide. In *Report of the Secretary's Task Force on Youth Suicide, Vol. 3: Prevention and Interventions in Youth Suicide.* Washington, DC: U.S. Department of Health and Human Services.

Golombok, S., & Tasker, F. (1996). Do parents influence the sexual orientation of their children? Findings from a longitudinal study of lesbian families. *Developmental Psychology, 32,* 3–11.

Gray, D., & Inensee, R. (1996). Balancing autonomy and intimacy in lesbian and gay relationships. In C. J. Alexander (Ed.), *Gay and lesbian mental health: A sourcebook for practitioners.* New York: Harrington Park Press.

Green, G. D. (1990). Is separation really so great? Special issue: Diversity and complexity in feminist therapy: I. *Women and Therapy, 9,* 87–104.

Hall, J. M. (1994). Lesbians recovering from alcohol problems: An ethnographic study of health care experience. *Nursing Research 43,* 238–244.

Kurdek, L. A. (1993). The allocation of household labor in gay, lesbian, and heterosexual couples. *Journal of Social Issues, 49*, 127–139.

Lockman, J. J. (1997, April). Discussion: Children born to lesbian mothers. Paper presented at the Society for Research in Child Development, Washington, DC.

Mays, V. M., Beckman, L. J., Oranchak, E., & Harper, B. (1994). Perceived social support for help-seeking behaviors of Black heterosexual and homosexually active women alcoholics. *Psychology of Addictive Behaviors, 8*, 235–242.

Martin, A. (1993). Adoption. In Martin, A. (Ed.), *The lesbian and gay parenting handbook: Creating and raising our families.* New York: HarperCollins.

Mattison, A. M., & McWhirter, D. P. (1987). Stage discrepancy in male couples. *Journal of Homosexuality, 14*, 89–99

McCandlish, B. M. (1987). Against all odds: Lesbian mother family dynamics. In F. W. Bozett (Ed.), *Gay and lesbian parents.* New York: Praeger.

McWhirter, D. P., & Mattison, A. M. (1996). Male couples. In R. P. Cabaj & T. S. Stein (Eds.), *Textbook on homosexuality and mental health.* Washington, DC: American Psychiatric Press.

Metz, M. E., Rosser, B. R. S., & Strapko, N. (1994). Differences in conflict-resolution styles among heterosexual, gay, and lesbian couples. *Journal of Sex Research, 31*(4), 293–308.

Patterson, C. (1994). Children of the lesbian baby boom: Behavioral adjustment, self-concepts and sex-role identity. In B. Green & G. Herek (Eds.), *Lesbian and gay psychology: Theory, research and clinical applications.* Beverly Hills, CA: Sage.

Patterson, C. (1995). Families of the lesbian baby boom: Parents, division of labor, and children's adjustment. *Developmental Psychology, 31*, 115–125.

Patterson, C. (1997, March) Children of gay and lesbian families: Research, law, and policy. Paper presented at Tulane University, New Orleans, LA.

Purcell, D. W., & Hicks D. W. (1996). Institutional discrimination against lesbians, gay men, and bisexuals: The courts, legislature, and the military. In R. P. Cabaj & T. S. Stein (Eds.), *Textbook of homosexuality and mental health.* Washington, DC: American Psychiatric Press.

Ramafedi, G., Farrow, J. A., & Deisher, R. W. (1991). Risk factors for attempted suicide in gay and bisexual youth. *Pediatrics, 87*, 869–870.

Reilly, M. E., & Lynch J. J. (1990). Power-sharing in lesbian partnerships. *Journal of Homosexuality, 19*, 1–30.

Rotherman-Borus, M. J., Hunter, J., & Rosario, M. (1994). Suicidal behavior and gay-related stress among gay and bisexual male adolescents. *Journal of Adolescent Research, 9*, 498–508.

Steckel, A. (1987). Psychosocial development of children of lesbian mothers. In F. W. Bozett (Ed.), *Gay and lesbian parents*. New York: Praeger.

6

Comparing Mixed-Race and Same-Sex Marriage

LOWELL TONG

*Taking a break along the journey down the road to
same-sex marriage, this chapter describes the parallel
journey made in the successful effort to overturn
laws that banned mixed-race marriage in the United
States. The struggle to allow mixed-race marriages
was very long and difficult, and it was not until
1967 that legal efforts finally overcame the resistance
of the remaining states that had anti-miscegenation
laws. The precedent of that 1967 case was evoked in
earlier efforts to allow legal same-sex marriage, but
the analogy between mixed-race and same-sex couples
was dismissed. Finally, with the Hawaii case, the
courts allowed the precedents of the mixed-race marriage efforts to apply to the current fight for same-sex
marriage.*

How is it that mixed-race marriages and same-sex marriages
have elicited such similar, strong reactions? Public, private, religious, social, and legal opinions in the 1940s to 1960s about
mixed-race marriage were contentious, vociferous, vehement, complex, and confusing. They led to the 1967 U.S. Supreme Court case,
Loving v. Virginia, which ended state laws prohibiting mixed-race

marriages. Opinions about mixed-race marriages were as hotly argued then as are the opinions debated now in the 1990s about same-sex marriage. This chapter examines both the controversies surrounding both types of marriage and the many similarities between them.

Race and gender are part of the core identity of anyone in Western society, and marital status carries extremely important traditional social functions and connotations. Just think how common it is to describe or think of someone by these attributes: a single Caucasian man, a married African American woman, or a widowed Asian American woman. In addition, marriage is considered to be one of the most important criteria of social organization in Western society. It has defined all manner of relationships from the interpersonal to dynastic, has provided a context for procreation, and contains deeply embedded moral, religious, and legal meanings.

BACKGROUND

It is no surprise, then, that the concept of marriage between untraditional pairings (for example, mixed-race in the 1950s or same-sex in the 1990s) is so controversial. After all, *untraditional* means new, different, and not initially expected in large numbers. We could expect guardians of tradition to have strong opinions about something seen by some as the potential upheaval of one of the very cornerstones of society itself.

Parameters of marriage have not been fixed over time. Marriage has not always been a legal contract between two consenting adults of opposite genders, even in the Western world. Marriage has been defined as primarily religious in some societies. It has been allowed between more than two people at the same time (polygamy and polyandry). It has been allowed between children (dynasty planning in Europe) and between an adult and a child (child brides). People have not always had the free choice of whom to marry (arranged marriages and picture brides). Even religious same-sex unions equivalent to marriage occurred in medieval Europe. Parameters of marriage, like any social phenomenon, have changed along with other social changes.

The historical debate over whether a white person in the United States should be legally allowed to marry someone of "five eighths Malay descent," as the following section describes, may sound somewhat quaint in the 1990s. Today, the thought of mixed-race marriage does not conjure charges of illegality and certainly not court-ordered punishment, though there still exist family and community objections based on racial or other prejudice. The concept of race itself has changed, from broad categories largely based on skin color and geography to the present-day categories based on culture, ethnicity, religion, and political boundaries in addition to skin color and geography. The concept of "five eighths Malay" would cause much confusion today: does this term apply to someone from Malaysia? The Thai part of the Malay Peninsula? The "East Indies"? Anywhere in Asia outside of China? Southeast Asia? What about someone from Sumatra, or Bali for that matter? How about someone of "pure" Cantonese ancestry whose family has lived on the Malay Peninsula for three generations? Or a Hindu Indian now living in Malaysia?

Perhaps thirty or forty years from now, the debate over same-sex marriage also will seem as quaint. Not only will marriage between two men or two women be a familiar occurrence, but attitudes and concepts about sexual orientation and gender roles will have changed. Perhaps the term *sexual orientation* itself will seem old-fashioned, as newer concepts of categories about gender, sex, love, and relationships take hold. Terms such as *lesbian*, *gay*, and *bisexual* may seem as antiquated, restrictive, or even as repressive as *Negro* and *colored*.

To make some sense of opinions on marriage, it is useful to consider three categories of opinion: social, religious, and legal.

Social opinion is difficult to quantify in the present and is an easy target for those who like to revise historical popular opinion in any direction. This chapter will not attempt to quantify popular opinion about mixed-race marriage or same-sex marriage. Instead, it will describe the range of personally held "popular" opinions about both.

Religious opinion is complicated by the fact that there are so many religions and their branches in Western society, including some that are not traditionally Western. There is a great range in personal adherence to religion, including no adherence to any religion at all. Personally held religious principles drive opinions and actions, which can coalesce into potent organized forces with the specific goal of shaping society.

Legal opinion is definitively and permanently recorded in two forms: federal and state legislation (known as laws or statutes) and published findings of court decisions. Many court opinions ponder and describe the social realities of the times, along with the intent of the scope and meaning of the laws, and therefore form a useful starting point for learning about social opinion.

ANTI-MISCEGENATION LAWS

The term *miscegenation* came into use in the United States by the latter half of the nineteenth century; its roots are the Latin *miscere* (mix) and *genus* (race). Other terms used to describe interracial marriage were *amalgamation* and *melaleukation*. These terms all described a type of marriage that was exceedingly rare, since it was sometimes illegal and in any event was counter to all social conventions. While some anti-miscegenation laws applied to specific racial mixes—some laws were originally intended to prohibit white and American Indian unions, for example—all laws were intended to prohibit marriages between whites and blacks. To examine anti-miscegenation laws is to examine racial discrimination and segregation in general and black-white race relations in particular. (A law prohibiting mixed-race marriages is an *anti*-miscegenation law. The term *miscegenation law* is sometimes inaccurately used in its place.)

Anti-Miscegenation Laws in the United States

While other countries in modern times have had laws banning mixed-race marriages, such as South Africa with its apartheid laws, the United States is considered to have had the broadest, most pervasive anti-miscegenation laws of Western-style democracies. In the United States, it is not the federal government but the states that regulate legal contracts such as marriage. Beginning in the white settlement and colonial periods and into the nineteenth century, states enacted and refined anti-miscegenation laws.

Virginia's anti-miscegenation laws arose during the period of slavery, when the strict definition and regulation of races were critical to the social and economic order of the day. California enacted an anti-miscegenation law in 1850, originally prohibiting (with criminal penalties) marriages between "white persons and Negroes or mulattos." There were subsequent revisions, including a transfer of the law into California's Civil Code and prohibitions against marriage between a white person and members of additional races such as "Mongolian" and "the Malay Race."

Anti-miscegenation laws uniformly prohibited marriages between blacks and whites but varied in which specific other combinations of couplings were actually prohibited, such as marriages between a white and a "Negro or Malay" in Maryland and marriages between a white and a "Negro or Indian" in Oklahoma and Louisiana. States varied in their definitions of *race*, using concepts such as the "five-eighths rule" or other percentages of predominant race (using parental and grandparental bloodlines to determine the percentage); and sometimes they did not define race at all. Because anti-miscegenation laws varied from state to state, it was possible for a mixed-race couple to be legally married in one state and be considered to have an illegal relationship (with punitive consequences) in another.

One small but important factor that led to the fall of state laws banning mixed-race marriages was that the definition of *race* itself was found to be vague, inconsistent, and technically impossible, as described in the "five eighths Malay" example earlier. It was also unclear whether the laws applied to marriage between people of any two different races or only marriage between a Caucasian and a non-Caucasian. Courts deciding against anti-miscegenation laws mentioned in their opinions that such laws were impossible to apply because of the controversy over what constituted race.

By the 1940s there was some movement to repeal anti-miscegenation laws, largely by declaring them unconstitutional. The first state to declare its anti-miscegenation laws unconstitutional was California (*Perez* v. *Sharp*, 1948). In 1957, thirty states still had laws prohibiting at least one form of mixed-race marriage, and in 1967, there were still sixteen states prohibiting marriages between "Negroes" and "whites" (*Loving* v. *Virginia*, 1967).

California Ends Its Anti-Miscegenation Laws

In the mid 1940s, a white woman, Andrea Perez, and a black man, Sylvester Davis, were refused a marriage certificate and license by the Los Angeles County Clerk, W. G. Sharp, on the basis of Civil Code statutes. These statutes stated, "no license may be issued authorizing the marriage of a white person with a Negro, mulatto, Mongolian or member of the Malay race." Perez and Davis took legal action, and their case was eventually heard by the California Supreme Court (*Perez* v. *Sharp*, 1948).

Perez, Davis, and their attorney, Daniel Marshall, argued that the statutes were unconstitutional because they prohibited the couple's right to religious freedom. Perez and Davis were Roman Catholics, and their religion had no rule forbidding them to marry as a mixed-race couple. They claimed that California statutes were denying them full participation in the sacraments of their religion by not allowing them to be married.

In considering religious freedom provided by the First Amendment to the U.S. Constitution, the court acknowledged that the state could regulate a marriage even if that marriage were within religious practices, since "freedom of conscience and the freedom to believe are absolute, [but] the freedom to act is not." However, the court reasoned that states could limit a religious "act" such as marriage only if "for the protection of society, and insofar as their regulations are directed towards a proper end and are not unreasonably discriminatory."

The court used monogamy as an example where the state could appropriately regulate marriage, even though it "might inhibit the free exercise of certain religious practices." Regarding the prohibition of mixed-race marriages, however, the court questioned whether miscegenation was really a social evil that warranted state legislative prohibition, or if an anti-miscegenation law were more "discriminatory and irrational, in which case it unconstitutionally restricts not only religious liberty but the liberty to marry as well."

The court declared that marriage itself is more than just a contract regulated by the state: marriage is a fundamental right. As such, marriage should not be prohibited "except for an important social objective and by reasonable means." It further declared that infringement upon such a right "must be based upon more than prejudice and must be free from oppressive discrimination."

The court noted that laws based on race alone had often been found, in other high courts, to be a denial of the constitutional right of equal protection. The historical exception to this was when a law was designed to combat a clear peril, as was the case during wartime emergencies. The court found that anti-miscegenation laws were "not designed to meet a clear and present peril arising out of an emergency." The court saw as its main determination "whether the state can restrict [a] right on the basis of race alone without violating the equal protection of the laws clause of the U.S. Constitution."

The court considered the argument that anti-miscegenation laws do not discriminate against any one racial group, since they apply to all persons regardless of race. The court declared that the question was "not whether different races, each considered as a group, are equally treated. [Instead], the right to marry is the right of individuals, not of racial groups."

The court examined California's anti-miscegenation laws in the context of other race-based statutes enacted at the same time and found them all to be discriminatory, racist, inconsistent, and arbitrary. For example, blacks and American Indians were forbidden to testify in state court for or against a white person. The court was aware of similar racist laws in other states that were based upon the assumption that people could be judged by race alone and that all non-whites were inferior to whites. The court also noted that anti-miscegenation laws were so arbitrary as to forbid the marriage between certain races but not others and also noted that it was impossible to define racial categories for many.

The court ultimately decided, in 1948, that anti-miscegenation laws were "the product of ignorance, prejudice and intolerance." The court instructed the Los Angeles County Clerk to issue Perez and Davis a certificate of registry and a license to marry.

The court, in summary, decided in favor of Perez and Davis on three main grounds: (1) Anti-miscegenation laws were invalid because they discriminated against persons of the basis of race or color and were not designed to meet a clear and present danger; (2) Anti-miscegenation laws arbitrarily and unreasonably discriminated against certain racial groups; and (3) Anti-miscegenation laws were too vague and uncertain for civil codes governing fundamental rights and liberties.

U.S. Supreme Court Ends State Anti-Miscegenation Laws

In 1967, the U.S. Supreme Court issued its landmark decision *Loving v. Virginia*, which effectively struck down all remaining state anti-miscegenation laws. Events leading to this case began in 1958, when Mildred Jeter, a black woman, and Richard Loving, a white man, both residents of the state of Virginia, decided to get married. They went to neighboring Washington, D.C., to get married, since they were legally able to marry there. The Lovings returned to Virginia as a married couple and established their home in Caroline County. Later that year they were indicted by a Virginia Circuit Court Grand Jury, which charged them with violating state anti-miscegenation laws. They pleaded guilty and were sentenced to one year in jail. The state trial judge suspended their sentence on the condition that the couple leave the state and not return to Virginia for twenty-five years. As cited in *Loving* v. *Virginia*, the state judge wrote, "Almighty God created the races white, black, yellow, Malay, and red, and he placed them on separate continents. And but for the interference with His arrangement there would be no cause for such marriages. The fact that He separated the races shows that he did not intend for the races to mix."

After their Circuit Court conviction, the Loving couple moved to Washington, D.C., and appealed their case to a higher Virginia court. They argued that Virginia's anti-miscegenation laws were invalid under the Fourteenth Amendment of the U.S. Constitution, which directs states "[not] to deny to any person within its jurisdiction the equal protection of the laws." The Lovings lost their appeal and took their claim to the highest state court, which again affirmed the convictions. The Lovings' case was then accepted in 1966 to be heard by the United States Supreme Court.

The Virginia laws dealing with mixed-race marriage explicitly prohibited any Virginia mixed-race couple who left the state for the purpose of a mixed-race marriage to return and live in Virginia as a married couple. The intermarriage of a "white person" with a "colored person" was a felony and both were subject to "be punished by confinement in the penitentiary for not less than one nor more than five years." Related Virginia laws defined "white" and "colored" persons; the Lovings never disputed that one was "white" and the other "colored."

The U.S. Supreme Court reviewed the State of Virginia's arguments that the state had "legitimate purposes . . . to preserve the racial integrity of its citizens, and to prevent the corruption of blood, a mongrel breed of citizens, and the obliteration of racial pride." The court noted that these arguments were clearly derived from the racist concept of white supremacy. The Supreme Court also reviewed the state's argument that the regulation of marriage was a matter to be left exclusively under state control. However, the court was compelled to note that a state's power to control marriages was not absolute and unlimited if that control were in conflict with the U.S. Constitution, including its amendments.

The Fourteenth Amendment

The first section of the Fourteenth Amendment to the U.S. Constitution, ratified in 1868, contains two clauses relevant to the *Loving v. Virginia* case: the equal protection clause and the due process clause. The U.S. Supreme Court examined whether Virginia's anti-miscegenation laws were compatible with these two clauses, the intent of the clauses at the time of their creation, and the way courts interpreted the clauses in other cases, including its own past cases.

Just as was argued by supporters of anti-miscegenation laws in the California case of *Perez v. Sharp*, the State of Virginia argued that the equal protection clause of the Fourteenth Amendment of the U.S. Constitution meant that penal laws with interracial elements were legal so long as they applied equally to different races. Because blacks and whites were equally punished in a mixed-race marriage, the state of Virginia held that there was no discrimination based on race, and therefore no violation of the Fourteenth Amendment "equal protection" clause.

The court, however, rejected the state's notion. "Mere equal application" of a law based on racial classifications did not satisfy the court's understanding of the Fourteenth Amendment's intent of "proscription of all invidious racial discriminations." Furthermore, the court rejected the state's argument that Congress never intended to void state anti-miscegenation statutes. The court declared the following: "There is patently no legitimate overriding purpose independent of invidious racial discrimination which justifies this classification. The fact that Virginia prohibits only interracial marriages involving white persons demonstrates that the racial classifications must stand on their own justification as measures designed to maintain white supremacy. We have consistently denied the constitutionality of measures which restrict the rights of citizens on account of race. There can be no doubt that restricting the freedom to marry solely because of racial classifications violates the central meaning of the equal protection clause."

The Supreme Court also found that Virginia's anti-miscegenation laws violated the due process clause of the Fourteenth Amendment. The court recognized that "the freedom to marry has long been recognized as one of the vital personal rights essential to the orderly pursuit of happiness by free men."

The Supreme Court summarized its judgment: "The Fourteenth Amendment requires that the freedom of choice to marry not be restricted by invidious racial discriminations. Under our constitution, the freedom to marry, or not marry, a person of another race resides with the individual and cannot be infringed by the state." It ordered that the Virginia convictions of the Lovings for being a mixed-race married couple be reversed.

SAME-SEX MARRIAGE LAWS

While the topic of same-sex marriage laws is covered in other chapters in this book, it is important to describe briefly the legal debate on same-sex marriage, so that it can be compared to the historical legal debate on mixed-race marriage.

Although there were previous attempts to recognize same-sex unions legally, a case heard by the Hawaii State Supreme Court, *Baehr* v. *Lewin* in 1993, is considered to be a landmark case. The State Supreme Court ruled that denying same-sex marriage was discriminatory and seemed unconstitutional because there did not seem to be any compelling state interest to override the unconstitutionality of discrimination. The State Supreme Court returned the case to the Circuit Court and asked the state to show, under a "strict scrutiny" standard, any compelling state interest to deny such marriages.

The case prompted, directly or indirectly, over thirty other states to consider or enact legislation banning same-sex marriages, in order to protect these states from having to recognize same-sex marriages that another state might legitimize. It also prompted the U.S. Legislature to enact the Defense of Marriage Act (DOMA), which defined *marriage* as a union between people of the opposite sex and allowed any state the option of not recognizing a same-sex marriage that might be allowed in another state. The Circuit Court concluded with *Baehr* v. *Miike* in 1996 that to deny marriage licenses to same-sex couples was in fact unconstitutional under the Hawaii Constitution.

Baehr v. *Lewin* also prompted the State of Hawaii to form a commission to examine the issue of same-sex marriage in the state. In 1995 the commission published its findings, which identified four basic reasons in support of conferring the benefits of marriage in total to same-sex couples: (1) the state and federal constitutional right to equal protection of the law; (2) arguments opposing same-sex marriage closely parallel arguments against mixed-race marriages in the *Loving* v. *Virginia* case, which were found to be unconstitutional; (3) a procreation requirement for marriage was invalid; and, (4) religious beliefs banning same-sex marriages should not be imposed by state law on those who do not subscribe to those beliefs.

COMPARING MIXED-RACE AND SAME-SEX MARRIAGE

Arguments on both sides of the debate over mixed-race marriage and same-sex marriage come from essentially the same core conflict: the struggle between change and preservation of the social structure. Into this struggle are brought arguments about civil rights, morality, victims, and the boundary between religion and government. Both debates attract arguments based on emotion rather than rational thinking, such as arguments regarding what is natural and what is not.

Mixed-Race Marriage

During the mixed-race marriage debate, society was on the verge of changing the way it formally regulated social divisions on the basis of race. U.S. race relations had been defined when whites first settled in America and expanded their territory by conquering Native Americans and their lands. Power and control by whites over blacks was firmly established during the period of U.S. slavery. In order to help validate the consolidation of power in those who already held it, white supremacy became the legal and social policy of the land. Well after slavery ended, lynching and other forms of physical violence and psychological terror continued to be employed to enforce racial power and control. Native Americans, blacks, and then other nonwhites, as well as some non-Anglo whites, had to be considered inferior in order to maintain the premise of white supremacy. Social mixing between races was limited, and the most egregious threat to race distinctions and segregation was interracial sex sanctioned through marriage. Mixed-race marriages not only meant a legal union but interracial sex and mixed-race children—and all three took on the connotation of a great evil. Mixed-race marriage was called abnormal, unnatural, and even against the intention of God.

In the anti-miscegenation case of *Perez* v. *Sharp*, opinions held by society were cited from the 1869 case of *Scott* v. *State:* "The amalgamation of the races is not only unnatural, but is always productive of deplorable results. Our daily observation shows us that the offspring of these unnatural connections are generally sickly and effeminate, and that they are inferior in physical development and strength, to the full blood of either race." Beliefs such as the mental inferiority of blacks to whites and the inability of mixed-race children to produce offspring were also documented in *Perez*

v. *Sharp*. These ideas, repulsively racist today, were part of firmly held public opinion.

In the 1990s, while some Americans might have racist-based ambivalence about a mixed-race marriage in their own family, most do not consider mixed-race marriages to be evil. The right to a mixed-race marriage is not considered to be a legal issue today, except by extreme racists. In some settings, especially cosmopolitan urban areas, mixed-race couples and mixed-race people blend in without particular notice.

Same-Sex Marriage

The debate about same-sex marriage is happening in the context of a society struggling to understand different sexual orientations.

How did homosexuality, the basis for same-sex marriage, come to be held as so unnatural, evil, or pathological? Marginalization, ostracism, and scapegoating of any group that is different and present in smaller numbers in comparison to the majority is a recurring social theme throughout history. Religious leaders and followers, especially of Judeo-Christian religions, have found pieces of evidence in their religious scriptures and traditional beliefs that they interpret as unambiguous evidence of homosexuality as sin, immorality, evil, or some other variety of bad and wrong. And from evidence derived from biased samples of lesbians and gays living in a world full of persecution and prejudice based on sexual orientation, "science" assigned homosexuality psychopathological status until the 1970s. Religion and science have not been granted immunity from general social prejudices.

There are those segments of society that firmly hold on to concepts about sexual orientation based on prejudice, fear, ignorance, and the elevation of tradition to moral superiority. People with such conceptions believe in heterosexual supremacy, which results in prejudice ranging from subtle attitudes to extreme behaviors. Heterosexual supremacy and heterosexism are potent factors underlying the physical violence, including murder and psychological terror, perpetrated toward people known or suspected of being lesbian or gay. *Gay bashing*, as such violence and terror is called, is related to the conscious and unconscious belief in heterosexual supremacy, just as black lynchings were the extreme result of racism and white supremacy. The concept of same-sex marriage can inflame existing prejudicial attitudes toward gays and lesbians. With legally sanctioned same-sex or mixed-race relationships, the unequivocal strength of marriage spans emotional boundaries, ranging from socially acceptable affection to the forbidden zones of intimacy and evil, unnatural sex.

There are those segments of society that have turned away from conventional beliefs reflecting the prejudice, fear, and ignorance related to heterosexism or heterosexual supremacy. Some of them have joined the Gay Civil Rights Movement, which began in the late 1960s and has championed gradual social, religious, scientific, and legal changes. There have been significant attitudinal changes towards the acceptance of lesbians and gays as full-fledged members of society. Some established religions and their offshoots have begun to acknowledge, accept, and even celebrate lesbians, gays, and their relationships. Mainstream U.S. scientific or behavioral health professional organizations no longer equate homosexuality with pathology. And in a number of cities and counties across the country, domestic partnership legislation has allowed same-sex couples some of the acknowledgment, rights, and responsibilities of married couples. But until same-sex couples are allowed to marry legally, their relationships hold second-class status.

Different Social Eras

Despite the fact that the debates over the two kinds of marriage began in two different social eras, there are many contextual similarities. Regarding differences, in the 1940s and 1950s, social rules related to race, gender, and sex were more formal, rigid, and strictly followed than they are in the 1990s. Geographic mobility was more limited, contributing to a slower spread of new ideas and less mixing of types of people. Jump to the 1990s and witness the Information Age, with instant global communication via television and the Internet, widespread domestic and international travel resulting in greater exposure to different people and ideas, and a greater acceptance of civil rights for minorities, including increased acceptance and even value of diversity in both workplace and community.

However, there also are significant similarities between the eras with respect to the debates on the two kinds of marriage. In the 1940s and 1950s, more mixing of whites and blacks began, partly a result of World War II and its impact on U.S. demographics. With this began an increase in opportunities for mixed-race socialization and, subsequently, marriage. The movement to end U.S. anti-miscegenation laws, beginning in the 1940s and ending with the *Loving* decision in 1967, coincided with the rising of the Black Civil Rights Movement, which many define as first realizing its full magnitude in the 1950s.

Compare this to the 1990s, an era of unprecedented "outing" of homosexuality. While the Gay Civil Rights Movement started in earnest at the end of the 1960s, it gained momentum and has hit its stride in the 1990s. Homosexuality is acknowledged and discussed more openly, as more gays and lesbians came out of the closet. As gays and lesbians confidently disclose their sexual orientation, they become, in turn, more confident about existing or new relationships. Long-term relationships between same-sex partners are coming out of the closet, with greater public awareness. Same-sex couples with children—either by former relationships, artificial or "natural" insemination, or adoption—are being acknowledged more publicly. Same-sex couples increasingly have begun to engage in commitment ceremonies and, where allowed, religious ceremonies and domestic partnerships—the only legal unions available.

The Comparison of Choice

Some people may say that the debates on the two types of marriage are not at all the same: one deals with a permanent and fixed characteristic not subject to choice (race), while the other has to do with a choice of "lifestyle" (sexual orientation). This position requires the belief that race is absolute and that sexual orientation is a choice. This argument, however, is really a smoke screen for underlying prejudice, fear, and hatred.

Race actually is not as absolute an attribute as commonly believed. One cannot change one's ancestors, but race is more than fixed ancestors—it also includes continuously changing definitions of subjective categories. U.S. Census reporting forms are one example; there seem to be more and different races and ethnic categories every decade. Statutes based on race distinctions have varied in their definitions of race: a person with five "pure" white great grandparents and three "pure" black great grandparents could historically have been considered "white" in one time and place, "black" in another, "colored" in yet another, or even "mulatto," based on mathematics alone, not to mention other subjective factors such as skin color or hair characteristics.

On the matter of sexual orientation and "choice," much has been written in this book and elsewhere about fundamental concepts of homosexuality, its "origins," its "nature," and discrimination and prejudice based on it. Two themes have emerged: (1) traditional views of homosexuality based on ignorance, assumptions, pathological models, prejudice, or stilted research are being replaced by nonjudgmental inquiry and objective experience; and (2) rigid, dichotomous views of sexual orientation are giving way to a more complex understanding of gender roles, sexual orientation, and sexual behavior. The concept of *sexual preference* has evolved to *sexual orientation*. Though still debated, it is now generally understood that while sexual behavior is subject to all sorts of circumstance and choice, basic sexual orientation is not.

While race and sexual orientation are obviously different descriptive categories, they are quite similar in that the choice factor breaks down for both, and, in their applications relevant to their respective marriage debates, neither is absolute.

CONCLUSION

What ties the debates on same-sex marriage and mixed-race marriage together is the struggle over the maintenance of traditional power and control. It is not surprising that Hawaii became the first state seriously to consider legalizing same-sex marriage. Hawaii is the most diverse state in terms of ethnicity, race, and religion, so there is much less domination by any one set of ideologies. There is already a long tradition of mixed-race marriages and offspring, and there are hundreds of different religions and denominations, including some that do not believe in God or only one God.

It should not be surprising, either, that single-ideology, conservative organizations oppose both same-sex and mixed-race marriages. For example, the Ku Klux Klan's seventh "political agenda," published in 1996, is to "outlaw homo-sexuality and inter-racial marriages." Reasons for advocating acceptance or rejection of mixed-race and same-sex marriages are remarkably similar.

The Fourteenth Amendment of the U.S. Constitution, Section 1, states: ". . . nor shall any state deprive any person of life, liberty, or property, without due process of law; nor deny to any person within its jurisdiction the equal protection of the laws." The equal protection clause does not explicitly mention race or gender, much less sexual orientation, but its principle of "equal protection" has been interpreted by the courts to extend to the principle of no discrimination based on race, sex, and other personal characteristics. In terms of same-sex marriage, high courts will ultimately have to decide that "equal protection" also applies to lesbians and gays, because it is the right thing to do—not uniformly right by all religions, nor right in the eyes of all majorities, but nevertheless right, given the context of the society in which we live. Gay men and lesbians must be treated with "equal protection" under the law of the land.

Same-sex marriage is as odd a concept now as mixed-race marriage was in the 1940s and 1950s. It takes time for people to get used to new kinds of marriage. Some argue that the very definition of marriage is that between a man and a woman, forgetting that the very definition of marriage used to be a relationship between two members of the same race. When the U.S. Supreme Court ordered the racial integration of schools with the 1954 case of *Brown* v. *Board of Education*, integration was not popular. So too, a legal ruling in favor of same-sex marriage may not be popular. Such a ruling, however, will be a huge advance for the civil rights of gay and lesbian people and may facilitate another type of integration—a greater acceptance of gay men and lesbians throughout society.

References

Baehr v. *Lewin*. (1993). 74 Hawaii 530, Supreme Court, State of Hawaii.

Baehr v. *Miike*. (1996). Civil Case No. 91-1394, First Circuit Court, State of Hawaii.

Boswell, J. (1994). *Same sex unions in pre-modern Europe*. New York: Villard Books.

Brown v. *Board of Education*. (1954). 347 U.S. 483, U.S. Supreme Court.

Gordon, A. (1964). *Intermarriage: Interfaith, interracial, interethnic*. Boston: Beacon Press.

Knights of the Ku Klux Klan. (1996, November 4,). http://members.iglou.com/kkk/belief.html.

Loving v. *Virginia*. (1967). 388 U.S. 1, U.S. Supreme Court.

Perez v. *Sharp*. (1948). 32 Cal. 2d 711, Supreme Court, State of California.

Scott v. *State*. (1869). 39 Ga. 321, State of Georgia.

State of Hawaii Report of the Commission on Sexual Orientation and the Law. (1995). http://kumu.icsd.hawaii.gov/lrb/soldoc.html.

United States Constitution, Amendment XIV. 1868.

7

Legal Trials and Tribulations on the Road to Same-Sex Marriage

GILBERT ZICKLIN

*Using a magnifying glass on the map of the road to
same-sex marriage, this chapter describes specific legal
cases and situations that have brought us to the
Hawaii case and to the verge of legally sanctioned
same-sex marriage. The journey is marked not just by
legal precedent or clear and objective judicial thinking
but by the biases and prejudices of the times. Changes
in the legal situation parallel changes in society's attitudes about gay men and lesbians.*

The meaning and import of marriage in Western civilization
have undergone significant change over the centuries. In the
long sweep of history, what made marriage central to culture and
social structure has shifted several times. If in certain periods marriage was essentially a financial arrangement between families; in
others it became mainly a religious sacrament; and in still others, a
sexually and emotionally intimate relationship. In our own historical era, marriage and family are portrayed as bastions of love and
security, as central to society, the very bedrock upon which our civilization is based. And even though the high-water mark of the pres-
tige of being married may have passed in the 1960s under the triple
assault of a rising divorce rate, the decline of suburbia as an ideal

living domain, and the feminist critique of gender roles, marriage still remains a gateway into social acceptability and carries a bevy of material advantages.

Indeed, marriage still occupies a privileged place both in our imagination and in our laws. A 1996 government study by the General Accounting Office found over one thousand references to special provisions for married couples in federal law and administrative codes. For this reason alone, any change in marriage laws as important as permitting same-sex marriage cannot simply arise from a sounder reading of the laws regarding who may marry. If such a change does occur, it will be in response to significant shifts in our culture with respect to the general acceptability of gays and lesbians. A more accepting culture will lead to more fair-minded legal decisions, not the other way around.

MARRIAGE AND GAY AWARENESS

Since Stonewall, the name we now give to the events that led to the present gay rights movement, marriage has become a salient issue for same-sex couples. For people who identified as gay and lesbian, belief in the equal moral worth of same-sex and opposite-sex relationships grew in proportion to the increasing self-confidence of the gay and lesbian community. In time, same-sex couples began to feel the sting of being denied the economic and moral benefits of state-sanctioned marriage, which their heterosexual counterparts took for granted. In the early 1970s, a few same-sex couples filed for marriage licenses, were administratively denied, and appealed to the courts for redress. Though nearly forgotten in the contemporary debates on gay marriage, these cases indicate the duration of the gay community's fight for recognition of their partner relationships. But the legal arguments made little headway with state and federal judges who, if they reflected American opinion on the matter, were unprepared to accept the moral and social equality of heterosexuality and homosexuality and therefore to revise the law regarding who may marry.

However, in the twenty-five years or so since these initial cases, knowledge and attitudes about homosexuality and about gay- and lesbian-identified people, have shifted significantly. In particular, a majority of the public now believes that gays and lesbians deserve protection from discrimination in the workplace, including the right to have one's partner included in one's insurance benefit. A majority also believes that gays and lesbians should not be barred from military service and that they can make good soldiers.

This shift in attitude is reflected in the 1993 Hawaii Supreme Court decision in *Baehr v. Lewin*. In this case, it was found that denial of a marriage license to same-sex couples constituted sex discrimination and therefore violated the equal protection provision of Hawaii's constitution. This is instructive, since this argument is similar to one that judges in earlier cases had rejected. *Baehr* highlights the possibility that it is not legal reasoning alone that is at work in deciding these cases but also the temper of the times. Indeed, as has been said, when significant shifts in legal interpretation are made, they do not reflect sudden discoveries of judicial error but rather reflect cultural changes. Examining the early cases along with *Baehr* will illustrate just such an interplay between cultural mores and legal decision making.

EARLY ATTEMPTS AT SAME-SEX MARRIAGE

As mentioned, there were several attempts on the part of same-sex couples in the 1970s to win the right to marry through litigation. *Baker v. Nelson* (1972) and *Singer v. Hara* (1974), decided in the appellate courts of the respective states of Minnesota and Washington, were among the more important of these early cases. In them, the petitioners for same-sex marriage relied on arguments based on constitutional guarantees of due process and equal protection, and, in *Singer*, the statutory and state constitutional language prohibiting sex discrimination.

Due Process

Taking up the due process argument first, the appellants asserted that the state's denial of a marriage license abridged the freedom of the individual to marry whomever he or she wants, within the limits set by the basic marital requirements (being of a certain age, unrelated, and so on). The freedom to marry had been articulated by the U.S. Supreme Court in a series of cases beginning in the nineteenth century; among the most recent in this line was *Loving v. Virginia* (1967), which struck down the state of Virginia's antimiscegenation statute barring mixed-race marriages. *Loving* bears particular scrutiny because the same-sex appellants referred to it prominently in their arguments.

In *Loving*, the court rejected the state's argument that outlawing interracial marriage was not racially discriminatory because the law denied such marriages to white and black persons alike. In rejecting Virginia's defense, the court concluded that while in its application it punished both white and black marital partners, the statute itself had "no legitimate overriding purpose independent of invidious racial discrimination."

Using *Loving* as a precedent, the appellants in *Baker* and *Singer* sought to convince the court that same-sex couples, like mixed-race couples, had the right to marry and that denying them this right was as arbitrarily discriminatory as denying it to mixed-race couples. But the courts did not acknowledge *Loving* as setting precedent for these cases. The courts argued that no right to marry was abrogated and that due process was not abridged since *marriage* by definition involved a relationship between two opposite-sex persons and that, therefore, the right to marry was simply not available to same-sex couples. Excluded by definition, same-sex couples could not claim that their constitutional right of due process had been abridged.

Equal Protection

In the same vein as in the due process argument, the courts in *Singer* and in *Baker* rejected the claim that withholding the right to marry from same-sex couples constituted denial of equal protection granted by the Fourteenth Amendment. The courts argued that since same-sex couples were unable to enter into marriage, they were not denied a benefit to which they were, in any sense, entitled. Moreover, even if marriage were not unavailable by definition, and gay and lesbian couples could conceivably marry, the state still might not be held in violation of equal protection for proscribing same-sex marriage. The equal protection doctrine makes allowances for the state's need to treat certain groups in society differently. While the courts have said that classifications based on traits used to discriminate against a group, such as race and, to a degree, gender, will automatically invoke a form of "heightened scrutiny," when it concerns other characteristics, such as sexual orientation, the court would only require that the state present a "rational basis" for its policy.

In *Baker* and *Singer* the rational basis consisted of the state's desire to grant privilege to opposite-sex marriage in order to foster and protect society's procreative institution. If the court had accepted the appellants' claim that distinctions in law based on the sex or sexual orientation of one's partner ought to be considered "suspect classifications," subject to "heightened scrutiny," then the state would have had to make a "compelling" rather than merely a "rational" case for its differential treatment of same-sex couples—a far more daunting undertaking.

Definition of Marriage

The appellants' analogy of their own fight against discriminatory marriage laws to that of *Loving* did not convince the judges hearing their appeal. In *Baker*, the court reasoned that "In *Loving* . . . the parties were barred from entering into the marriage relationship because of an impermissible racial classification. There is no analogous sexual classification involved in the instant case because appellants are not being denied entry into the marriage relationship because of their sex; rather . . . because of the *recognized definitions* [emphasis added] of that relationship as one which may be entered into only by two persons who are members of the opposite sex."

In accepting "recognized definitions" of marriage as the basis for preventing same-sex couples from marrying, the court relied on a clear tautology: same-sex couples cannot marry because, according to the "recognized" (that is, traditional) definition, they cannot. Of course, the court was free to find that the "recognized definitions" of marriage violated the rights of same-sex couples and could have ordered the definition amended. This action would have been analogous to the Supreme Court's finding that the state of Virginia's traditional ideas about race and marriage violated constitutional rights.

The failure to find in favor of the same-sex couples' arguments, and, in the process, to lift the moral status of gays and lesbians, had as much to do with their already low standing in society as with legal reasoning. One need only look at the language used in certain decisions stemming from that period to see in what disfavor homosexuality was then held by some jurists. For example, in *McConnell v. Anderson* (1972), a case involving the withdrawal of a job offer to a librarian who had sought to marry his same-sex partner, a federal judge wrote, "It is . . . a case . . . in which the prospective employee demands . . . the right to pursue an activist role in *implementing* [emphasis in original] his unconventional ideas concerning the societal status to be accorded homosexuals and, thereby, to foist tacit approval of this *socially repugnant concept* [emphasis added] upon his employer."

IMPROVED STATUS OF GAYS IN SOCIETY

By the 1990s, public acceptance of homosexuality and the public's support for certain of the rights of gays and lesbians had undergone significant change. The new, more tolerant attitude may underlie the striking difference between the Hawaii Supreme Court's *Baehr v. Lewin* decision and the *Baker* and *Singer* decisions.

The Hawaii Case and Discrimination

In *Baehr*, a majority of judges found that the way a lower court applied the Hawaii marriage statute violated the equal protection rights of same-sex couples and was invidiously discriminatory. They found that the Hawaii Constitution's equal rights amendment prohibiting sex discrimination pertained to this case, since they took the sex of the appellants, as opposed to their sexual orientation, as the determining factor in their being denied a marriage license.

Obviously, finding in favor of the appellants on the basis of sex discrimination, rather than on the basis of sexual orientation discrimination, avoids the issue of sexuality altogether, since heterosexually orientated same-sex partners could marry under this rubric. Strictly speaking, then, the decision isn't an affirmation of sexual orientation identity (that is, gayness) at all; but it seems it is being read this way, since it will be of greatest use to gays and lesbians. Still, the affirmation of sex rather than sexual identity is significant for future legal work.

With sex the issue, the court then argued for a "heightened scrutiny" standard of review for determining whether a permissible classification was made in refusing same-sex couples a marriage license. This meant that the state could only justify its classification of same-sex couples as ineligible to marry by showing *a compelling state interest*, rather than just a *rational basis*, for its decision.

While the *Baker* and *Singer* courts rejected the analogy with *Loving*, the court in *Baehr* accepted it. The plurality found bogus the lower court's argument that excluding same-sex couples from marriage was not sex discrimination because both men and women were equally forbidden from marrying persons of the same-sex. Citing the Supreme Court's decision in *Loving*, the court wrote,

[T]he Virginia courts declared that interracial marriage simply could not exist because the Deity had deemed such a union intrinsically unnatural, 388 U.S. at 3, 87 D.Ct. at 1819, and, in effect, because it had theretofore never been the "custom" of the state to recognize mixed marriages, marriage "always" having been construed to presuppose a different configuration. With all due respect to the Virginia courts of a bygone era, we do not believe that trial judges are the ultimate authorities on the subject of Divine Will, and, as *Loving* amply demonstrates, constitutional law may mandate, like it or not, that customs change with an evolving social order.

The court's decision in *Baehr* may be no more legally astute than those of *Baker* or *Singer,* though it is certainly more sympathetic to gays and lesbians. Could the *Baehr* court's interpretation of what constitutes unlawful sex discrimination derive as well from what it felt was morally required in the case, and culturally permissible, as from their reading of the state constitution? The point, again, is that courts do not rule in a social vacuum; the perception of the moral standing of the litigants may, at times, be as important as their arguments in the application of the law. Witness the historic shift of the Supreme Court on "separate but equal," which was seen in 1896 as acceptable, but sixty years later was overturned. In 1993, in Hawaii, the moral standing of the gay and lesbian community might have made their unequal treatment seem significantly more invidious and less tolerable than it had been a generation ago.

The Hawaii Case and Compelling State Interest

In its decision, the Hawaii Supreme Court required the government to show that its use of sex as a basis for granting or withholding marriage licenses was necessary for achieving a *compelling* state interest and advised the lower court to rehear the case on this basis. The rehearing took place in September 1996. Three months later the judge ruled that the state had failed to show that excluding same-sex couples from marriage was necessary to achieving a compelling state interest and ordered the state to grant marriage licenses to the appellants, pending an appeal by the state. The case was heard under the new name of *Baehr v. Miike.*

As of this writing, the situation in Hawaii is rather fluid with respect to the possibility of gay marriage. Hawaii House and Senate members are grappling with whether to amend the Constitution in such a way as to avoid the consequences of *Baehr* altogether and to accommodate same-sex couples by putting some kind of domestic partnership into effect instead. Should the Supreme Court reject the state's appeal of the latest trial court decision, as seems likely, and should the two legislative houses fail to agree on a compromise or substitute, then the court will order the state to grant marriage licenses to same-sex couples.

BACKLASH IN THE UNITED STATES

The very possibility of same-sex marriage has provoked a political backlash well beyond the borders of Hawaii. Backlash is not a phenomenon known only to gays and lesbians. When minority groups make gains that move them closer to equality with the majority, a backlash can develop, especially from those whose social standing and material well-being are affected or perceived to be affected by the minority's gains. Unlike the gay rights movement, however, the backlash spawned by successes of the civil rights and women's movements did not have the support of institutions such as the churches, whose mission is to uphold society's central ethical and moral values.

Influence of Churches

In the case of the lesbian and gay movement most churches are either against it or neutral; few are the movement's allies. The backlash against gays and lesbians can be more open and more extreme because it does not have to come up against the organized and influential opposition of the religious community nor any other reasonably powerful institution in shaping public opinion.

State and Congressional Backlash

The opposition to gay rights by influential institutions is why state legislators, state attorneys general, and a majority in the U.S. Congress have been able to mount such a quick assault on the right of gays and lesbians to marry. They have passed legislation and announced rulings asserting that a Hawaii same-sex marriage will not be recognized as a valid marriage.

The full effect of such a move will depend upon whether or not the "defense of marriage" acts, as they are sometimes called, and the corresponding attorney general rulings, are determined to be in violation of the "full faith and credit" clause of the Constitution. Article IV, Section 1 of the Constitution provides that "full faith and credit shall be given in each state to the public acts, records and judicial proceedings of every other state."

CONCLUSION

As of this writing, legal scholars are debating under which conditions, if any, one state can refuse to honor the judicial proceedings of another state, and whether the Defense of Marriage Act passed by Congress and signed by President Clinton, which authorizes states to refuse to recognize a same-sex marriage licensed under the laws of another state, is constitutional. If and when Hawaii does grant marriage licenses to same-sex couples, the U.S. Supreme Court may be called upon to decide whether or not other states must treat such couples as legally married.

As before in the process of rectifying the degradation of a minority group, an essentially political decision will be presented in terms of a legal-rational argument. Hence it is crucial for the partisans of the minority group to recognize that such decisions are, in the main, the outcome of political and cultural movements that convey the justice of the minority's cause. In that sense, the decision in Hawaii is a representation, however imperfect, of the efficacy of those movements.

References

Baehr v. Levin, 825 P.2d 44 (1993).
Baehr v. Miike, 1996 WL 694235, 1996 Haw. App. LEXIS 138
(Haw.Cir.Ct., 1st Cir.).

Baker v. *Nelson*, 191 N.W.2d 185 (Minn. 1971), appeal dismissed, 409 U.S. 810 (1972).

Boswell, J. (1980). *Christianity, social tolerance, and homosexuality.* Chicago: University of Chicago Press.

Leonard, A. S. (1997, February). Marriage pot boils in Hawaii. *Lesbian/Gay Law Notes,* 9–10.

Loving v. *Virginia*, 388 U.S. 1 (1967).

McConnell v. *Anderson*, 451 F.2d 193 (8th Cir. 1971), cert. denied, 405 U.S. 1046 (1972).

RAND Corporation. (1993). *Sexual orientation and U.S. military personnel policy: Options and assessment.* Santa Monica: Author.

Singer v. *Hara*, 522 P.2d 1187 (Wash. Ct App. 1974).

Zicklin, G. (1995). Deconstructing legal rationality: The case of lesbian and gay family relationships. *Marriage & Family Review, 21*(3/4), 55–76.

8

Ceremonies and Religion in Same-Sex Marriage

DOUGLAS C. HALDEMAN

An important part of the journey toward same-sex marriage has been the parallel efforts to address this rite of passage in religious institutions. Most of the current and best-publicized struggle for same-sex marriage has been for civil marriage—a right granted by the government. Many organized religions, though, have begun to look at recognizing same-sex relationships or even ritually sanctioning such marriages. Many gay men and lesbians who are religious or spiritual have sought the blessing of organized religion. Many couples have created and performed their own commitment ceremonies, akin to marriage ceremonies. This chapter looks at this road and the personal journeys of several couples.

Seattle's summer is said to start after the Fourth of July; those who plan outdoor events do so at their own risk. But this Fourth was perfect: big, billowy clouds against the backdrop of a cerulean blue sky, and a gentle breeze off Puget Sound. The guests began to arrive in the early afternoon, in silks, linens, and picture hats. A casual observer might have thought that the attendees, strolling through the carefully tended yard, had come for an elegant summer garden party. But the three-tiered cake in the center of the buffet table, topped with two small male dolls and the inscription "Long may they wave," was a dead giveaway that this was not going to be your ordinary garden party.

It was the summer of 1980, that window of time in gay history between the hypersexualized seventies and the advent of the health crisis of the eighties and nineties. After managing a long-distance relationship for a year, my partner and I decided to wed on the Fourth of July. The date was chosen as symbolic of freedom: the freedom that we felt in starting a life together; the freedom that we felt to acknowledge this to our friends and family. To have a self-designed, homemade wedding celebration seemed to be a natural extension of the way in which we experienced our relationship: that we would not be isolated but would live our married life in a social context of extended family and community.

At the time, lesbian and gay weddings were uncommon and never the focus of media attention. We had no idea how the world at large might view our celebration in the garden. Moreover, we knew that many of our lesbian and gay friends would criticize our ceremony as heteromimetic; still, for us, it seemed unquestionably right. As two gay men who came out in the seventies, we recognized the importance of social support. It was our intent to establish a stronger bond with our chosen community by publicly acknowledging our love and our lifetime commitment.

We celebrated with neither church nor officiant. For me, this did not diminish the spiritual impact of the day. Upon reflection, though, I see that it had never even crossed my mind to involve organized religion in our wedding, so scalded had I been by the hot splashes of guilt-inducing religious structures. At the time, we did not see our ceremony as revolutionary; it rather served to affirm publicly that which already existed—a marriage in the true sense of the word, even if not in the legal sense.

SPIRITUALITY AND CEREMONIES IN THE LITERATURE

Many years have passed since my partner and I exchanged vows on that uncharacteristically sunny Fourth of July. During that time, the topic of same-sex marriage has captured national attention and sparked considerable debate. There is a growing literature on the topic, from perspectives of law and society, history, and cross-culturalism. A book by Becky Butler in particular provides an intimate look at a variety of lesbian couples who have chosen to marry. Lesbian and gay couples planning a wedding may now consult guides specifically written for them or engage the services of wedding planners and consultants.

The ceremonies of same-sex marriage may serve both practical and spiritual functions. Letitia Peplau describes several myths about lesbian and gay relationships. Perhaps the one that receives the most tabloid-style promotion from anti-gay groups is that homosexuals do not desire and are incapable of achieving lasting relationships. Paradoxically, those most invested in this myth also are those most opposed to same-sex marriages, as if they are afraid of being proven wrong. It is impossible to speculate what the stability of same-sex relationships would be if they were legalized; however, in Denmark, where same-sex domestic partnerships have been legally registered since 1989, the "divorce" rate for lesbian and gay couples is below that for heterosexual couples.

The spiritual and religious aspects of same-sex marriage, however, have received minimal attention. This parallels the trend in mental health aspects of lesbian, gay, and bisexual experiences, in which spiritual and religious concerns tend to be marginalized. The reasons for this are twofold: first, spiritual experience is difficult to quantify and as such has been generally neglected in mainstream psychology and psychiatry. Second, organized religion has historically been indifferent at best, and actively hostile at worst, to lesbians and gay men. The prospect of addressing spiritual and religious concerns becomes somewhat akin to venturing into enemy territory.

Furthermore, the heteromimetic quality of lesbian and gay marriage rites is a legitimate concern for many who disavow heterocentrism or the institution of marriage altogether. For such couples, same-sex marriage ceremonies are not only irrelevant but evocative of an oppressive heterosexual culture. Often, it is the ceremonial aspects of same-sex marriage that are the most controversial within the lesbian and gay community itself. Gay-affirmative theologians, in their writings, have tended to focus on affirming the viability of spiritual expression or challenging the traditional anti-gay interpretations of scripture used by fundamentalist Christians to justify bias, discrimination, and sexual orientation conversion therapy.

Same-sex marriage ceremonies have received scant documentation. The importance of ritual, however, is undeniable for many. Same-sex couples who choose a ritualized form of union tend to experience marriage as a cultural universal, the natural expression of all whose love has deepened to a lifetime commitment. For them, the celebration of marriage is not the sole property of heterosexuals but a valued and ultimately liberating expression of a lifelong commitment for all who love. The anti-gay positions taken by many religions can create in some a generalized aversion to anything that smacks of ceremony or ritual. But for others, surviving institutionalized anti-gay hostility can actually create a need for anchoring that is met by ritualistic expression. Of these ritualistic anchors, the marriage ceremony is perhaps the most meaningful and moving.

Those writers who do attempt to address the ceremonial aspects of same-sex marriage do so with a keen observer's eye. These writers are able to reveal what a variety of same-sex marriage ceremonies are like, which factors are taken into consideration in the planning, how the issues of family of origin and chosen family are addressed, even what attire is chosen. What is lacking in the literature, however, is an analysis of the meanings underlying such events.

WHY A CEREMONY?

In contrast to describing the ceremonies, the focus here is more clinical or existential in nature. The primary objective of this chapter is to provide a deeper understanding of the psychological and spiritual meanings associated with same-sex marriage ceremonies.

The answers to the question, Why have a same-sex marriage ceremony? vary from couple to couple, but two common themes emerge. One has to do with the desire for a public context for the enactment of a marriage ritual, so that the community of extended family may bear witness to and actively support the couple's life commitment. In the absence of legal recognition, this aspect of ceremony becomes doubly important. Second are the more individual needs for spiritual and religious expression. These may vary significantly from person to person, and within couples some compromises and adjustments may need to be made based upon different spiritual views. However, all of the couples presented in this chapter acknowledge the ceremony as an opportunity for spiritual expression of one sort or another, from the traditional to the innovative.

The couples presented in this chapter approached their respective ceremonies with thoughtfulness and care, as most heterosexual couples would. For lesbian and gay couples, there is the additional overlay of social opprobrium. Heterosexual couples plan their weddings in a context that assumes normalcy. Even if the respective families of origin do not get along or disapprove of the match, there is still the social sense that the ceremony follows a normative path. For the lesbian or gay couple, in addition to focusing on the details of the event itself, there is also often the added worry of how the most joyous moment of their lives may be viewed negatively by family members. Will my parents come? Will they share this with their own friends? The heterosexualization of marriage adds great complexity to the lesbian or gay couple contemplating a marriage ceremony. Whether or not it is the couples' intent, social oppression inevitably politicizes most lesbian and gay weddings, simply by virtue of their public nature.

The Wedding: 1993

The Reverend Troy Perry, founder of the Metropolitan Community Church, the nation's first gay church, conducted a mass "wedding" for two thousand couples in conjunction with the 1993 March on Washington for Lesbian, Gay and Bi Equal Rights and Liberation. Reverend Perry, in his address to the couples, stated, "We stand before our nation and our friends because we wish to proclaim our right to love one another. We stand here knowing that love makes a family—nothing else, nothing less! We stand here knowing of the lies and untruths that have been told about us by some in the larger community. But we stand here pure of heart and unafraid in proclaiming that our concern and care for one another is as rich as that in any culture or community."

"The Wedding," as it was called, exemplified one of the themes common to lesbians and gay men who marry: the need for community support. It further provided probably the most graphic example to date of the fact that lesbians and gay men do in fact seek to make permanent their relationships and that they are based on values of mutual love and respect. Such relationships thus become normalized in the eyes of those who would otherwise be unaware of their existence, were it not for the public demonstration of commitment.

Spiritual Identity for Gay Men and Lesbians

Other answers to the question, Why marry? are more personal in nature. The meanings associated with spiritual experience and expression for lesbians and gay men has been described by a variety of authors, including myself. Gay theologians, in their analysis of the unique factors underlying spiritual issues for lesbians and gay men, refer to a "wound" suffered at the hands of a stigmatizing, hostile society. In a model proposed by Harvey, the wound is caused by the infection of shame, fear of abandonment, and feelings of worthlessness, which are transmitted by a homophobic society. More traditional gay theologians have used different language but similar concepts in presenting models by which social rejection severs the connection between the lesbian or gay man and the structures in the external world. This process turns the individual's attention inward, enabling the person to access and develop her or his inner spiritual resources.

Corollary to this is the concept of spiritual identity. Many lesbians and gay men who experience rejection at church walk away from organized religion and never look back. Still others, so repulsed by the vendetta against lesbians and gay men of many fundamentalist Christian churches, categorize all organized religions as enemies. But for reasons unclear, some lesbians and gay men experience their identity as imbued with a spiritual aspect that is both important and indelible. Such individuals cannot live fully integrated, satisfying lives apart from some kind of spiritual and/or religious practice. Further, they may suffer rejection at church for being gay and ridicule among their gay peers for being religious. Nonetheless, the attachments that can be formed with religious institutions, even those that are ambivalent about homosexuality, can be quite powerful.

Potential Harm from Organized Religion

Lesbians and gay men are at risk for a variety of mental health problems when they attach to churches or religious organizations that actively promote negative views of homosexuality. Such institutions are often attractive to shame-ridden, depressed individuals who have been exceptionally vulnerable to familial and social rejection. Feeling ashamed and sinful, many hyperreligious gay men and lesbians gravitate toward programs such as "Homosexuals Anonymous," "Exodus," and "Love in Action," all of which promise a "cure" of homosexuality—and a new, acceptable, heterosexual life—through prayer and group support. The social pressure for some to accomplish the daunting task of eradicating homosexual fantasies and changing sexual orientation is enormous.

Very often, such individuals leave "treatment" feeling even worse about themselves for having failed to become heterosexual.

Religious expression, or lack thereof, has a wide range of implications for lesbians and gay men. The spectrum ranges from outright rejection of religion and spiritual practice, which is an adaptive and healthy response for many lesbians and gay men, to spiritual practice that is more amorphous and nontraditional in nature, to a strong identification with a religious or spiritual community. All of these perspectives are valid; it is only when religious practice adheres to prejudicial and unscientific views of same-sex sexual orientation that the lesbian or gay person is at risk for psychological harm. The Bible is for many a powerful agent of both society and history, and it can be used as a force for punishment as easily as it can be used for growth.

ORGANIZED RELIGION AND SAME-SEX MARRIAGE

For the lesbian or gay couple seeking to affirm a covenant relationship within the context of an organized religious tradition, the choice of denomination may be determined by personal history and/or current religious affiliation on the part of one or both parties. Alternatively, both parties may self-identify as spiritually inclined, in the broader sense of the term, but not be active participants in any religious congregation or spiritual community. In such cases, the couple may agree on a more secular ceremony officiated by a person with spiritual or religious credentials. Very often, such a cleric may be affiliated with a spiritual community that is favorable to the idea of same-sex marriage ceremonies. Most lesbian and gay couples who choose to have a commitment ceremony seek either a central or peripheral religious element therein. This section briefly reviews the position taken by many communities of faith toward same-sex marriage.

Metropolitan Community Church
Verses Other Churches

For lesbians and gay men seeking to ritualize a marital commitment in a Christian context, an obvious alternative is the gay Metropolitan Community Church (MCC). Theologically, the MCC defines marriage as "a covenant relationship between two individuals." Since its founding in 1968, the MCC has performed about two thousand "holy unions" a year. Several liturgies are available for such ceremonies.

For some, however, the desire to wed within one's church tradition or simply to receive the sanction of a mainline denomination can be compelling. Mainstream religious organizations maintain a wide range of positions on lesbian and gay identity and same-sex marriage, though few are openly supportive and affirming.

The majority of mainline Protestant denominations (Episcopal, Presbyterian, Lutheran, Methodist) periodically become embroiled in highly charged discussions about the ordination of openly lesbian and gay clergy, but so far only one has given official sanction. The United Church of Christ (Congregationalist) has had a nondiscriminatory policy relative to openly lesbian or gay clergy since 1972. To date, the conservative Baptist and Pentecostal denominations have not considered the issue. Debates about the fitness of openly lesbian or gay individuals to serve as clergy are invariably divisive, serving to remind lesbian/gay churchgoers and the public at large that these institutions are at best places of uneasy tolerance. At the same time, most of these denominations have some congregations that have chosen to self-identify as open and affirming to lesbians and gay men.

Affirming Protestant Denominations

Not all Protestant denominations are ambivalent or hostile to lesbians and gay men, nor are they necessarily rejecting of lesbian and gay couples seeking covenant blessing. The United Church of Christ, mentioned earlier, is home to numerous ministers who reject an interpretation of biblical scripture as proscribing lesbian or gay identity or same-sex marriage. One such minister, the Reverend John H. Mack of the First Congregational United Church of Christ in Washington, D.C., put it this way: "[I]t is extremely easy to interpret the profound teachings of our religious scripture to apply to same-sex relationships. It is extremely difficult to find clear condemnation of them within the religious literature. And the systemic persecution of those who find romantic love with a person of the same sex violates virtually every major law and teaching of both Judaism and Christianity."

Since 1984, the Unitarians have conducted services of holy union for lesbian and gay couples. The Reverend Scott W. Alexander of Boston's Unitarian Universalist Association states, "While such [lesbian and gay] unions are not yet recognized by civil authorities, our church recognizes and sanctifies them with the same authority and affirmation we do for a heterosexual marriage. The only difference in our tradition is that when the union being performed is between a heterosexual man and woman, the minister conducting the service is obliged to sign a marriage license and return it to local authorities. Unitarian Universalists are working in our society to ensure that someday gay and lesbian couples will receive the same recognition and support of their committed, caring, and loving relationships."

Similarly, a number of Quaker meetings have affirmed same-sex couples' parity with heterosexuals as regards marriage. There are even cases of fundamentalist pastors performing same-sex unions, though these are decidedly the exception to the rule. Citing the lack of scriptural support for the prohibition of such unions, some fundamentalist pastors have stated that lesbians and gay men deserve the opportunity, through marriage, to sanctify their relationships and commit to a moral standard that they are often accused of being incapable of maintaining.

The Catholic Church

These examples notwithstanding, the Christian churches' positions on same-sex marital unions is at best a mixed bag. The official position of the Roman Catholic Church is explained in the "Letter to the Bishops of the Catholic Church on the Pastoral Care of Homosexual Persons," written in 1986 by Cardinal Ratzinger. The Church characterizes homosexual orientation as "a strong tendency toward an intrinsic moral evil" and denounces any expression thereof. This position, along with the church's teachings that human sexuality in general is only appropriately expressed in procreative sexual activity, has driven multitudes of lesbians and gay Catholics from the pews. Still, a Catholic upbringing being what it is, not all lesbian and gay Catholics choose to leave the church. Many progressive Catholic clergy have adopted the views expressed by Father James Mallon of Philadelphia's Dignity congregation.

A Vatican II document, *Gaudium et Spes* (Pt. II, Ch. 1) describes marriage as "not merely for the procreation of children . . . in cases where despite the intense desire of the spouses there are no children, marriage still retains its character of being a whole manner and communion of life." Father Mallon further defines marriage as "the ultimate form of friendship achievable by sexually attracted persons." In this definition, heterosexual orientation is not interpreted as being a prerequisite. Since Rome's position is that the homosexual person has a right to an "intimate, lasting, supportive, and maturing friendship," Father Mallon, in his pastorate, has offered same-sex couples the option of holy union ceremonies.

It could certainly be argued that the intent of the Catholic Church hierarchy is seriously stretched in the foregoing. Nevertheless, the position taken by Father Mallon offers a safe harbor for those lesbians and gay men who are compelled to sail the stormy seas of Roman Catholicism.

The Episcopal Church

Described by comedian Robin Williams as "Catholicism lite—all of the ritual, but only half the guilt," the Episcopal Church does not maintain an official position on homosexuality or on same-sex unions. However, a number of progressive Episcopal parishes have been the site of same-sex marital celebrations. One such celebration in 1996 featured the full marriage liturgy in conjunction with a high mass, celebrated by the dean of an archdiocesan cathedral. The ceremony was attended by several hundred people, including numerous city officials and the governor of Washington.

Interestingly, this couple had eighteen months previously been refused the right to celebrate their union in the cathedral by the bishop, necessitating the last-minute cancellation of a large and elaborately planned wedding. So strong was the couple's commitment to each other and to their community of faith that they persevered in their campaign to persuade the bishop that the two, parishioners of the cathedral parish, should be united in their chosen home of faith. Ultimately, permission was granted for the dean to proceed as he saw fit.

The resulting ceremony was as moving as it was memorable. As one of the attendees, I can say that the sight of two men as full participants in the holy union liturgy, with which I was very familiar, added a new dimension to my own spiritual experience: for the first time in years, I felt that I actually belonged in my own church.

Judaism

While Judaism does not offer a unitary view of same-sex relationships, there is ample precedent for some, particularly Reform congregations, to be supportive. Rabbi Yoel H. Kahn of San Francisco's Congregation Sha'ar Zahav addresses the question of whether or not Jews can endorse *kiddushin* (usually translated as "sanctification") for the marriage of same-sex couples, given that their relationships cannot be based upon procreation. Rabbi Kahn suggests that homosexual relationships cannot be held to a different standard than heterosexual ones and that, like many same-sex relationships, some heterosexual relationships do not produce children.

Further, he points out that the same-sex couple who has children from one spouse's previous marriage, chooses adoption, artificial insemination, or surrogacy to fulfill the Jewish responsibility to parent is really not so different from the heterosexual family who does likewise. In his discussion of Reform Judaism's commitment to affirming the responsibilities of the individual, Rabbi Kahn advocates a "plurality of expressions of covenantal responsibility" in which "different Jews will properly fulfill their Jewish communal and religious responsibilities in different ways."

Congress last year passed the Defense of Marriage Act, which affirms the right of states not to recognize same-sex marriages performed in other states, in a preemptive strike against the Hawaii case. This action implies that same-sex unions somehow threaten the institution of heterosexual marriage. Given the number of states that have passed such bans, this fear appears to be widespread. Rabbi Kahn addresses this issue as follows:

> I do not believe that encouraging commitment, stability, and openness [of same-sex relationships] undermines the institution of the family—it enhances it. At present, many gay and lesbian Jews are estranged from the synagogue, the Jewish community, and their families of origin because of continued fear, stigma, and oppression. Welcoming gay and lesbian families into the synagogue will strengthen all our families by bringing the exiles home and by reuniting children, parents, and siblings who have been forced to keep their partners

and innermost lives hidden. *K'lal yisrael* [the community and unity of the Jewish people] is strengthened when we affirm that there can be more than one way to participate in the Covenant.

SPIRITUALITY AND CEREMONIES IN PRACTICE

Four couples who have made their vows in a same-sex marriage ceremony were gracious enough to share their stories with me. They are presented here to provide anecdotal supplement to the social and spiritual concepts relevant to same-sex marriage. These couples were not randomly selected for interview, nor are they intended to be viewed as representative in any way of lesbians and gay men who marry. Their stories are offered so that the reader may connect the foregoing material with the marital experiences of real people. I wish to acknowledge my gratitude to all four of the couples for offering their stories with such love and generosity.

David and Peter—July 1, 1994

David and Peter are both ministers in the United Church of Christ (Congregationalist) (UCC) and met while in divinity school. Peter had self-identified as gay for some time, but it was not until meeting Peter—and ultimately falling in love with him—that David came to a similar awareness within himself. The couple early on had made a private commitment to a covenant relationship and envisioned a lifetime together.

Peter states, "A relationship cannot be sustained by two people alone." After the couple had been together for eight years, the time seemed right for a more public expression of their covenant, as part of a worship service that included their family and friends. David and Peter were married in a UCC church, using the standard wedding text from the marriage ceremony they both had performed many times. They wrote and adapted their own vows for use in the ceremony. Peter notes that the public recitation of marriage vows invites a promise from the community to support the relationship.

Those members of the community most central to the celebration of David and Peter's wedding were their respective families of origin. It was important to both of them that their families be present, witnessing their vows and physically standing behind them. David notes that not all same-sex couples have families who are willing to participate in their weddings. For them, he suggests that the church can serve as a substitute family. David described one lesbian couple who belong to his congregation. These women did not have family members who were willing to attend their wedding, so several of the women from the congregation stepped in as surrogate mothers. These women saw to the details, both practical and psychological, that biological mothers normally would tend to for their daughters.

Enacting their vows "in the presence of God" was perhaps the most central element of all in David and Peter's wedding. Both characterized their public commitment as an expression of their striving "to be the most faithful, honest people that we can be," and this means acknowledging their relationship in the context of faith. Both also noted that the connection to an ancient tradition was an important aspect of their marriage ceremony.

Although they had been together eight years when they married, both David and Peter reported that the relationship felt different after the ceremony. The process of making public a promise before God somehow made the relationship more real, more solid. The cohesion of an already strong bond intensified through the process of marriage; as David put it, "This is not something I have to worry about ending tomorrow." In addition to sharing a marital life, the two are both on the pastoral staff at a large UCC church.

Cathryn and Connie—October 1, 1994

The first thing a visitor to Cathryn and Connie's beautifully appointed home sees is a plaque in the entryway that bears their marriage vows and the signatures of the 125 guests who attended their wedding. The road to that day, which they describe as having been a "holy moment," was forged from both deep love and significant struggle.

The two met at a professional conference; Connie was a corporate executive and Cathryn a consultant. The two describe a first year long-distance relationship characterized by intense attraction, though the two came to the relationship from different life experiences. Connie had self-identified as lesbian long before meeting Cathryn; the recognition that she was the great love in her life came early in their acquaintance. While the recognition was similarly strong for Cathryn, the identity matrix into which the relationship would fit was different. Cathryn had not been lesbian-identified prior to meeting Connie; the resulting integration of this new relationship was challenging. Cathryn described it as a balance scale, which forced her to weigh her self-concept as a "good girl"—who lived to meet the expectations of others—against the love she felt for Connie on the other side. A person of faith and an ordained Presbyterian minister, Cathryn initially thought that God was on the side of the "good girl." Further, she had thought she was happy in traditional roles expected of women: wife, mother, caretaker. Ultimately, her revelation was that she did not have to be the "best little girl in the world"; in fact, she could stop living her life for everyone else—a position her family of origin came to support.

After one year together, Connie proposed that they marry. Two and a half years passed from that point until the actual wedding. The couple reports that Cathryn's two children, from a previous heterosexual marriage, were instrumental in their decision. Said Cathryn's eleven-year-old son to Connie: "You're not my real stepmom until you get married." The relationship between the couple and the father of Cathryn's children had been difficult and continues to be so. Further, Cathryn's family of origin (Connie's is no longer living, save for one brother) has demonstrated a wide range of responses to the couple, from wholehearted acceptance to shame and embarrassment. Connie reports that "all of the events in our life have been an act of faith; a 'letting go.'"

The couple was unable to find a church that was willing to marry them or to find other clergy who would help them. Interestingly, this caused more fascination than anger or disappointment. As an alternative, the couple decided to marry in their wooded and beautifully landscaped back yard. They did not put a great deal of effort into the trappings of the wedding, concentrating instead on the spiritual aspects. They both indicated that a lesbian/gay wedding has one advantage: like gayness itself, you are going outside expected tradition, so you are free to make up your own script. Bearing this in mind, the couple honeymooned in Hawaii prior to the wedding.

Cathryn and Connie both state that they had "gained the right to marry" and that God was in attendance—along with 125 human guests, ranging in age from four to eighty, representing all races and sexual orientations. Afterward, both reported feeling "more settled; more sure." And as regards the lack of legal recognition or social benefits of a lesbian marriage, Cathryn states, "The marriage is more important because I get no benefits. I didn't do it for any social gain. I did it because I would stake my life on my love for her."

Much has been written about gay men as sexual beings. Seeking sexual variety was the primary hallmark of liberation for gay men in the seventies; it implied freedom from heterocentric constraint that was irrelevant to the lives of gay men. Little, however, has appeared in the literature about gay male courtship. When this becomes a topic of interest, Grant and John's story would make a valuable contribution.

Grant and John—October 13, 1996

Grant and John met at a time when they were both ready to consider a relationship but were in no rush to become deeply involved. Grant, in particular, had seen himself as having moved too quickly in past involvements and so was committed to allowing time for his relationship with John to develop. In contrast to the way in which many gay relationships begin from a sexual basis, Grant and John decided to get to know each other before exploring the sexual dimension of their relationship. In part, this was because they wanted to move slowly, but also because they wanted to rescript their experience of sex to include love and emotion in addition to eroticism.

As is the case with many couples, Grant and John were not exactly on the same time schedule. John reports being ready to propose marriage sooner than Grant, but recognized so many wonderful qualities in him that it was not an issue to wait until Grant was ready. John admired Grant's thoughtfulness and caution and so was never impatient with the process. Ultimately, both agreed that having a marriage ceremony was important, in large part due to the importance both place upon family. It was important that they celebrate their commitment publicly.

Another added benefit of marriage for Grant and John had to do with the ceremony itself and the exchange of vows. They took a year to fully develop the ceremony, a process that helped define the relationship more clearly. They became engaged two and a half years prior to marrying. A year following their engagement, a friend hosted an engagement party for them, which included most of both men's families of origin. Grant manifested some anxiety about this event, especially about how the public acknowledgment of their commitment would be received. John, on the other hand, reports staying calm and relaxed, and both men note that the party served as a prelude to the wedding itself. Many supportive, moving statements were made by friends and family.

John's parents were overwhelmingly supportive of the couple; Grant's mother was also, but Grant's father had a more difficult time initially and did not attend the engagement party. He did, however, attend the wedding and is now getting closer to the couple.

The excitement of planning the wedding spanned a full year. The couple attended a wedding exposition; they contacted three of every vendor, ultimately selecting one. The spiritual aspect of the wedding was an item for negotiation, as Grant wanted the spiritual part of his identity to be addressed, and John wanted no mention of either God or Jesus. They ultimately asked a Unitarian minister to preside as officiant, since her tradition's "secular humanism" appealed to both of them. The minister met with them in their home and was able to fashion a ceremony that was appropriate for both of them by integrating aspects of their similarities and differences.

The minister invoked the blessing of Grant and John's families and friends thus: "The ceremony in which we are now participating is a bold, even a revolutionary act. We pray that men who love men will one day be free to celebrate their love openly, in every aspect of their lives. In the meantime, we can express the joy and approval we feel for Grant and John as they give public recognition to the love they feel for each other and the commitment they freely make to one another today. Let me therefore ask all of you assembled here to rise. In a moment, I'm going to ask you to affirm Grant and John's relationship with a big 'We do!'" The spiritual aspects of the ceremony were further conveyed by the couple's choice of music.

John reports that since marrying Grant, he experiences recognition as a married couple from friends, family, and co-workers. He states that "people see us differently; I expect people to respect us." Grant feels that marriage has brought the relationship a sense of permanence; he senses an enhanced security with the knowledge that he and John will be able to work through whatever issues emerge.

The couple now has new projects to work on. They are in the process of buying a home, in their typical fashion—with a great deal of forethought and planning. The couple also hopes to adopt a child sometime in the next two years. There is no doubt that marriage has changed their lives. Grant calls it "the biggest outing I've ever been through."

Lynn and Margaret—April 13, 1996

To understand the marriage of Lynn and Margaret, it is necessary to have some understanding of the Quaker tradition into which they were both born. The Society of Friends, or "Quakers" as they are nicknamed, is a nonhierarchical spiritual community whose presence in this country goes back to the seventeenth century. Lynn's ancestors came to America in the 1600s, fleeing religious persecution in Europe. She is in the twelfth generation of a Quaker family; her parents are multigenerational in the same meeting (the name Quakers use for their congregations). Margaret is from a second-generation Quaker family. For both of these women, the importance of continuity with history in the Quaker tradition appears to be very deep-rooted.

The primary tenet of the Quaker faith, as Lynn and Margaret describe it, is that "there is that of God within each person." The focus of the spiritual community, then, is how to understand God's call and to respond accordingly. The four "testimonies" (roughly equivalent to principles) in the Quaker tradition are peace, simplicity, equality, and community. There is no formal liturgy and there are no clergy.

Quaker meetings (also the term for the gathering itself) are leaderless; they occur in a silence that is broken only when someone experiences God having spoken to them, at which point the individual speaks. Decisions are made in "unity," which means that the meeting as a whole, after a process of "threshing" (involving testimonies and discussion), feels called to move in a particular direction. At present, the issue of parity for lesbian and gay couples is a primary topic in many Quaker meetings, although the meetings function independent of one another. Some heterosexual couples feel so strongly about the issue that they themselves have declined to marry until lesbians and gay men also have the right to do so.

Lynn and Margaret met through the Quaker community in early 1993. The first year of their relationship was conducted via long distance. Both brought significant resistance to the idea of marriage. Lynn had experienced a bias against the institution itself, feeling that it was for heterosexuals. Coming from a conservative East-coast family, Lynn felt certain that, were she and Margaret to marry, her family would not attend, which would render the occasion pointless. Both Lynn and Margaret had previously made lifetime marital commitments that they subsequently broke, and neither relished the prospect of the same thing happening again.

However, as time passed, the two realized that the relationship strengthened over time. Ultimately, as Margaret's children began to observe that they were in reality already married, they began to inquire about when they would actually formalize the commitment. Both felt led by God to marry and so, according to Quaker custom, sought support to do so from their meeting's Committee on Oversight. Lynn and Margaret wrote their own vows, in consultation with the meeting's Arrangements Committee. They both felt that vowing life-long commitment was an invitation to divorce, so this standard component of wedding vows was omitted from their ceremony. The Quaker vision of marriage is that the couple is married by God, not a representative. Lynn and Margaret recited the following statements at their meeting for marriage: "to be honest and faithful, to care for (thy) well-being, to take each other's family as (our) own, and to help (thee) answer God's call in (thy) life." And Lynn's family did attend the wedding, which was followed by a sit-down dinner for two hundred. In keeping with the Quaker tradition of simplicity, the guests were fed salmon, which a fisherman patient of Margaret's had given them in exchange for treatment.

The changes brought about by the marriage were profound. In one way, the event itself was simply a recognition of what already existed; but in another way, it created a sense of parity and inclusion for both of them. Margaret now feels "on a par" with her heterosexually married siblings. Lynn now feels herself to be part of the mainstream, after a lifetime of feeling ostracized. She speaks of her marriage to Margaret in terms of what it means to "join the flow of humanity, of the family since 1650. I'm not a splinter. I'm part of it; and that happens partly through marriage."

CONCLUSION

This chapter is not a comprehensive assessment of the psychosocial underpinnings of lesbian and gay marriage ceremonies. Given that this territory is relatively uncharted, the intention of this work is to stimulate dialogue and provide direction for future study of the issue. I would therefore hesitate to draw definitive conclusions about the meanings of same-sex marriage ceremonies; however, I suggest that the anecdotal information reported both in the literature and in the stories of the couples interviewed for this chapter provides certain common themes.

The most significant common theme for same-sex couples who marry has to do with *connection to family and community*. In every case, the marriage ceremony was described as being central to the couple's ability to embed their commitment in a social context. For some, the primary factor associated with this sense of community was family of origin.

A corollary to this value is that of *public witness*. All of the couples described in this chapter felt that their relationships could not be fully honored without the public declaration of marital vows, so that the community would have the direct experience of the couples' commitment. Most of the couples reported that following their weddings, they experienced an enhanced sense of internal cohesiveness as a result of their public declarations. Further, several reported the experience of being perceived differently in society; as stable and permanent, "on a par" with heterosexually married people, as Lynn put it.

Familiarity, along with history and tradition, both cultural and religious, were essential for some of the couples in the experience of the marriage ceremony. For others, particularly those distanced from families of origin because of being lesbian or gay, the primary value is placed upon chosen or extended family. In any case, these marital relationships do not exist in vacuums but rather in the context of community. As Peter stated, "A relationship cannot be sustained by two people alone."

Spiritual expression was a third universal quality in these same-sex marriages. The ceremonies ranged from traditional to nontraditional, but to all of these couples, the opportunity to pledge their vows met their needs for spiritual experience. Most of the couples identified this as sanctifying their relationships in the presence of God, though some reported a more generic, less traditional spiritual context. These weddings ranged in style from elaborate to very simple; but however much attention the couples paid to the outward details, all of them, in their own ways, considered the spiritual aspect of their vows as central to the event itself.

It should also be noted that when children were a part of the relationship, the formalizing of a marital commitment on the part of the parental couple was an enhancement of the children's experience of family. In the cases described in this chapter, the children actually urged their same-sex parents to marry. This may not be a general trend, but it suggests a useful area for further research, particularly given that lesbian and gay couples are so often vilified as having a harmful effect on children.

I suppose that many heterosexually married couples would look at the foregoing themes relative to same-sex marriage and feel that their own experiences of what makes a marriage ceremony important are mirrored therein. To greater or lesser extent, these themes are universal aspects of ceremonial marriage. But what is different about lesbian and gay weddings? *Struggle*.

These marriage ceremonies are enacted in spite of, not because of, the sociocultural context in which they occur. In order to marry a person of the same sex, an individual must first overcome her or his own homophobic attitudes and challenge what is often a disapproving family, community, and society. This speaks not only to the strength of the couples' inner psyches but to the strength of their commitment. As Cathryn said, "I didn't [marry her] for any social gain. I did it because I would stake my life on my love for her."

References

Boswell, J. (1994). *Same-sex unions in pre-modern Europe*. New York: Vintage Books.

Bouldrey, B. (1995). *Wrestling with the angel: Faith and religion in the lives of gay men*. New York: Riverhead Books.

Butler, B. (1997). *Ceremonies of the heart: Celebrating lesbian unions*. Seattle: Seal Press.

Cherry, K., & Sherwood, Z. (1995). *Equal rites: Lesbian and gay worship, ceremonies and celebrations*. Louisville, KY: Westminster John Knox Press.

Eskridge, W. (1996). *The case for same-sex marriage: From sexual liberty to civilized commitment*. New York: Free Press.

Haldeman, D. (1996). Spirituality and religion in the lives of lesbians and gay men. In R. P. Cabaj & T. S. Stein (Eds.), *Textbook of homosexuality and mental health*. Washington, DC: American Psychiatric Press.

Harvey, A. (1992). *Hidden journey: A spiritual awakening*. New York: Arkana/Penguin Books.

Helminiak, D. (1994). *What the Bible really says about homosexuality*. San Francisco: Alamo Square Press.

Peplau, L. (1993). Lesbian and gay male relationships. In L. Garnets & D. Kimmel (Eds.), *Psychological perspectives on lesbian and gay male experience*. New York: Basic Books.

Scanzoni, L., & Mollenkott, V. (1978). *Is the homosexual my neighbor? Another Christian view*. New York: Harper and Row.

Thompson, M. (1994). *Gay soul: Finding the heart of gay spirit and nature*. San Francisco: HarperCollins.

9

International Trends in Same-Sex Marriage

LESLIE GORANSSON

The final stop on this exploration of same-sex marriage allows us to back up and see the journey from a global perspective. While the best-known and most widely publicized efforts have been here in the United States, many other countries have undertaken the same type of journey but with roads that have followed different landscapes and roadmarkers, based on the culture and politics of the countries in question. This chapter reviews the successes and failures to legalize same-sex marriages around the world and concludes with lessons that will be of help for those of us who are still carving out and laying down the final section of the highway to same-sex marriage in the United States.

*I*n the last several years, many gay men and lesbians have shifted the focus of their individual relationships and of their political work toward seeking the right to marry. An outgrowth of the battle for civil rights, the discussion of the right of gay people to marry has now become a significant political issue internationally. No countries to date have provided gay men and lesbians with the right to marry. There are, however five countries that allow gay men and lesbians to register their partnerships and gain some of the same rights and protections married people receive: Denmark, Greenland (as part of Denmark), Norway, Sweden, and Iceland. Hungary has recently allowed common-law marriages to apply to gay men and lesbians.

BACKGROUND

In 1989, Denmark enacted the Registered Partnership Act, which provided same-sex couples with almost all the legal rights of heterosexual couples. The act only applies to same-sex couples, and at least one partner must be a permanent resident of Denmark and a Danish citizen. The main rights excluded from the act are the right to insemination services and adoption. Danish divorce law governs the dissolution of a registered partnership.

Norway and Sweden followed in 1993 and 1994, respectively, and Iceland passed its registered partnership legislation in 1996. The Norwegian and Swedish laws echo the Danish law. The Icelandic legislation expands on the Danish legislation, as the following text describes. Partnerships registered in Denmark, Norway, Sweden, and Iceland are not recognized outside of their home countries. However, as these couples travel to other European Union member states as tourists and for employment opportunities, they are increasingly likely to request that other nations recognize their personal unions.

Differences exist between the Scandinavian concept of registered partnership and the U.S. concept of domestic partnership. Registered partnership in Scandinavia is the result of national legislation, while domestic partnerships are municipal matters. Registered partnership confers most of the rights, advantages, and responsibilities of marriage, whereas domestic partnerships usually simply confer insurance benefits or the right to visit one's partner in the hospital or in jail.

The cultural differences between the countries that have approved same-sex registered partnerships provide a critical backdrop against which to consider the legislative processes that occurred in these countries. Although the outcome—legal rights for lesbian and gay male couples—may be similar, the distinct national values and belief systems that motivated the change are important determinants in achieving those legal rights. For this reason, the experience of these nations cannot necessarily be transferred to the United States. The primary lesson they offer, however, is that understanding the cultural context of our own nation, our values and belief systems, will be essential to achieving equality. Given the cultural diversity of the United States and the strong tradition of individual states' rights, achieving such equality will be a daunting task.

This chapter focuses primarily on the experience in the countries that have achieved partnership legislation and describes the cultural influences and political processes that led to these historic achievements. In addition, the chapter summarizes the situation with countries progressing toward same-sex marriage and those opposed to the idea.

COUNTRIES WITH NATIONAL SAME-SEX PARTNERSHIP LEGISLATION

An impressive number of countries now heads the list of nations considering the rights of gay men and lesbians to join together in legally recognized and, to some degree, culturally sanctioned relationships.

Denmark

Denmark will always have the distinction of being the first country to legally recognize same-sex partnerships. For that reason, cultural and political factors will be examined, along with the ultimate effect of the law.

Cultural Factors

When the Nazis occupied Denmark in World War II, they ordered the mayor of Copenhagen to force Jewish residents to wear identifying yellow stars. The mayor instructed *all* citizens, regardless of religion, to wear the yellow stars. The citizens willingly complied. This historic example illustrates that Danish culture is built on a solid humanist foundation with a firm, pervasive commitment to benevolence and tolerance.

The Danish state church is itself democratic, with popularly elected parish councils, and is characterized by a tradition of freedom and commitment to humanism. As Nikolai Grudtvig, a popular and influential Christian thinker in nineteenth-century Denmark said, "Human being first and then a Christian." Denmark's cultural identity as a place of tolerance no doubt provided the historical backdrop for breaking the bounds of heterosexual tradition and enacting the modern world's first legal recognition of same-sex relationships.

Beginning in the 1960s, Denmark experienced a cultural revolution like the one that occurred in the United States, although perhaps with broader acceptance. In Denmark, as growing numbers of women entered the workforce, unconventional forms of cohabitation became increasingly popular, such as collective living communes and group families. The media were interested in and drew much public attention to the new collective living lifestyles. These forms of cohabitation made a little more headway among homosexuals in the 1970s than among heterosexuals, but there was a strong positive cultural opinion connected with the new ways of community living.

Marriage laws in Denmark historically emphasized that married couples consist of independent individuals, each of whom has rights over his or her own property and income, and that neither of them is responsible for obligations entered into by the other. However, they have "mutual maintenance obligations"; that is, no matter who the breadwinner is, each has financial responsibility for the other. Somewhat inconsistently, the woman was allowed to a certain extent to purchase everyday necessities at the man's expense, although the man could not act in a similar way. This custom was gradually considered discriminatory against the woman, making her dependent, and in homosexual circles was used as an argument against seeking "marriage."

Political Factors

Danish civil servants in the ministries and elsewhere have considerable influence on public opinion. At the same time, members of Parliament are influenced not only by the voters but also by interest groups and by the mass media. The organizations that raise, explain, and present an issue clearly to the public and politicians have a relatively good chance of getting their views accepted in Denmark.

In 1968, the Socialist People's Party (SF) sought to provide legal status for the newly emerging forms of cohabitation and presented a bill to revise the Marriage Act. The basis of the proposal was that people arranged their lives in many different ways, many of which were far removed from the traditional pattern of the nuclear family. The bill was not adopted, but a committee was appointed to look into the broader consequences of and the ideas behind the SF proposal.

In 1973, the committee rejected the idea of marriage for gay men and lesbians, because it would mean a breach with the traditional view of marriage and might have an unfortunate effect on other countries' evaluations of the validity of Danish marriages. The committee report, "Cohabitation Without Marriage," published in 1980, stated that the committee did not wish to create a framework for registration of cohabiting same-sex couples but rather was interested in solving "isolated legal problems concerning cohabitation." They indicated willingness to consider amending certain relevant laws at a later date to resolve these legal problems.

Denmark's National Organization for Gay Men and Lesbians (LBL) took a different approach. Three potential strategies were developed to approach the authorities: (1) request equality with heterosexuals (either marriage or the compete abolition of marriage); (2) create a special framework for cohabitation providing the same legal rights as heterosexuals; or (3) broaden some of the legal effects of marriage to apply to the cohabitation of same-sex couples. The third approach was raised largely because of objections to the mutual maintenance obligations in the existing marriage act. In 1975, the LBL concluded that the gay and lesbian community was no longer interested in a heterosexual-type marriage and therefore focused on the third strategy. In 1978, LBL introduced the concept of a "partnership" having certain legal effects and including "public registration of lasting cohabitation" as a parallel to marriage.

LBL prepared a detailed proposal including very thorough research into the effect registered partnership might have on existing marriage laws. The proposal, which was adopted by LBL in 1981, attempted to explain and address as fully as possible both the legal and economic problems that arose for same-sex couples and models for the solutions. It also made clear that it would not find a "second-class marriage" acceptable. The proposal provided for the same legal effects as heterosexual marriage, addressing such issues as housing, pension, inheritance, deaths, and divorce. It did not grant the right to adopt children—neither a partner's children nor unrelated children.

In May 1984, the Danish parliament mandated a commission to "elucidate the social circumstances of homosexuals in Denmark." The commission produced interim reports that directly influenced concurrent legislative initiatives. For example, the antidiscrimination legislation was extended to include a prohibition against discrimination on the grounds of "sexual orientation" as well as sex, race, and religion. Thus, antidiscrimination laws protecting the rights of individuals preceded the legal protection of same-sex couples.

Danish parliamentary practice changed during the 1980s, allowing for majority votes on single issues to pass, even if the votes were against the presiding minister or government. Opposition parties could now collaborate with interest groups and possibly get the recommendations of the minority carried through to a decision by a parliamentary majority without the support of the government. Although the majority initially rejected the LBL proposal of a law on "registered partnership for two persons of the same sex," the LBL was later able to lobby successfully and convinced the members of Parliament to vote away from the party line, resulting in a decisive majority supporting the measure.

The law came into effect on October 1, 1989, with two remaining problems: homosexuals were not yet permitted to adopt children, and the new legislation did not require the state Lutheran church to offer gay-marriage ceremonies. Nonetheless, the first registrations took place at the town hall in Copenhagen on the same day. In May 1997, twelve bishops of the Danish State Lutheran Church approved a report that sanctions same-sex unions in the church but characterized them as "dissimilar" to heterosexual marriages. The church stipulated that a different ceremony would have to be followed for gay marriages.

Effects of Same-Sex Partnership Legislation

Although the registration law creates a bond enforceable in law, it does not provide the same rights as marriage between men and women—same-sex couples were not granted access to adoption, artificial insemination, in-vitro fertilization, or church weddings. Also, one partner in the registered couple must be a citizen and live in Denmark.

A review of the first seven years of registered partnerships (through January 1, 1996) for Danish lesbian and gay male couples shows that 2,083 unions had taken place, 70 percent of them between men. Of these unions, a total of 17 percent of these couples have divorced—14 percent of gay men in registered partnerships compared to 23 percent of lesbian couples. Over 10 percent of these partnerships (219 in total), practically all of them between men, ended with the death of one spouse.

Initially supported by an estimated 60 percent of the population, partnership opponents had warned that the law would draw gay men and lesbians from around the world into their country and undermine and diminish an institution historically intended for heterosexuals. Even some gay men and lesbians opposed the law for philosophical reasons, saying partnerships shouldn't be modeled after heterosexual marriage. They called for equality through individualized contracts not tied to love, religion, or tradition.

Today, most politicians and government officials apparently consider the partnership law a success, believing it enhances the country's reputation and gives committed same-sex couples improved protection and legal status. Economic benefits include drawing more than thirty thousand visitors to Copenhagen in the summer of 1996 for Europride, an annual European festival for gay men and lesbians. Per Stig Moller, a Christian Democrat member of Parliament who abstained from voting on the issue in 1989, now concedes that foreign homosexuals have not, as feared, transformed the solemn Danish marriage ceremony into a circus in a rush for registration. Instead, the law has helped stabilize Danish homosexuals in committed relationships by offering status and extending rights. "Now they live officially," he said. "It works."

The adoption of Denmark's registered partnership law has resulted in much greater visibility and acceptance for gay men and lesbians, both in Denmark and abroad. For example, all Danish government forms now must include questions about partnership as well as marital status. Internationally, the Danish partnership law affected and inspired similar legislation in other Scandinavian countries. While celebrating the landmark legislation, many Danish gay men and lesbians believe that the law will not be fully satisfactory until the right to adopt children or have a wedding is included.

Throughout the process in Denmark, it appears that the seemingly simple act of beginning the debate eventually led to significant changes in legislation. Much of the social change that has occurred in recent decades in the United States has occurred not through Congress (our parliamentary equivalent) but through litigation. (Witness the processes on issues such as abortion, same-sex marriage, and assisted suicide.) Are the courts as influenced by public opinion as representative government bodies appear to be? Is the U.S. judicial system less influenced by prejudice than the court of "public opinion"? The social tolerance that is the pride of Danish culture may have allowed a different process of acceptance than may be possible in United States.

Greenland

Greenland and the Faeroe Islands (north of the Shetland Islands, near Norway) are self-governing external territories of Denmark. As such, Greenland voted in 1994 to ask the Folketing (Danish Parliament) to extend the 1989 law to Greenlanders, which they did.

Norway

For several years preceding passage of Norway's partnership legislation in 1993, a committee representing gay organizations lobbied Parliament for such legislation. Ultimately, five members of Parliament (from different parties) introduced partnership legislation based on the Danish precedent. Aina Hauge, a member of the gay committee, states, "Even though many within our organizations wanted adoption rights as well as artificial insemination, it was clear that a law containing that wouldn't pass. Therefore that was not included."

Norway passed its registered partnership legislation on April 1, 1993. The legislation provides for national insurance benefits, pensions, and inheritance and mandates the mutual responsibility of couples to support each other financially. The law passed the Odelsting chamber of the Norwegian parliament by a vote of 58 to 40 on March 29 and the Lagting chamber by a vote of 18 to 16 on April 1. There was strong opposition from several religious groups.

Sweden

Homosexuality was decriminalized in Sweden in 1944. Apparently, the politician who championed decriminalization had a gay brother who had experienced blackmail or knew of gay men who had been blackmailed, and he successfully put forth one of the first modern decriminalization laws.

Surveys conducted in Sweden in the mid 1980s by Per Arne Hakansson showed that many homosexuals nonetheless continued to experience significant discrimination. The surveys also revealed that over half of Sweden's citizens did not believe that two people of the same sex should be allowed to get married. At the same time, just under half replied "yes" to a question on whether homosexuals living together should be able to obtain loans in order to purchase a home.

In 1984, a commission appointed by the Swedish minister of social affairs submitted its report investigating discrimination against homosexuals in Sweden. The commission's report paved the way for the nation's anti-discrimination law of 1987, a domestic partner law in 1988 (a long-standing law that previously covered only same-sex couples), and ultimately, the Swedish Registered Partnership Law, which became effective on January 1, 1995.

Sweden's parliament enacted registered partnership legislation for gay men and lesbians on June 7, 1994, by a vote of 171 to 141, with 5 abstentions and 32 absences. At the time, Prime Minister Carl Bildt stated, "We accept homosexual love as equivalent to heterosexual. Love is an important force to personal as well as social development, and should therefore not be denied." As in Denmark and Norway, the Swedish law granted same-sex partners all the rights of marriage except access to adoption, artificial insemination, in-vitro fertilization, and church weddings. Also, in all three nations, one partner must be a citizen living in his or her home country. All foreigners seeking partnership with a Swedish citizen must already be permanent residents of Sweden at the time the partnership is registered.

Since Sweden legalized gay partnership, more than four hundred same-sex couples have registered—75 percent of them male. In Sweden, the cohabitation of gay men and lesbians can be regulated either by the domestic partner law or the registered partnership law, though as a gay or lesbian domestic partner one has less legal protection than a registered partner does. (For example, a domestic partner does not automatically inherit a deceased partner's assets, as a registered partner does.)

Iceland

The Icelandic parliament passed a resolution in 1992 creating a government committee to explore the legal, cultural, and social condition of homosexuals in Iceland and to propose legislative measures to abolish discrimination. In 1994, the gay issues commission recommended that Iceland legalize gay and lesbian marriage, criminalize discrimination against homosexuality, and substantially increase education about homosexuals in schools. The majority of the committee recommended adopting laws similar to those in Denmark, Norway, and Sweden. The committee minority, comprised of members from the Icelandic Organization of Lesbians and Gay Men, urged the adoption of more expansive laws that would completely equate heterosexual and homosexual relationships.

On June 4, 1996, the Icelandic parliament, Althingi, passed the partnership laws recommended by the committee, with one opposing vote and one abstention. The laws took effect June 27th, on International Gay Pride Day at the request of Samtoekin '78, Iceland's national gay and lesbian organization. On that day, Samtoekin '78 organized a reception at the City Theater, inviting all members of Samtoekin '78 and their friends and families, all members of Parliament, the mayor of Reykjavik and the City Council, human rights activists, the press, and others. The guests of honor were the nation's first "married" gay couples and the president of Iceland, Vigdis Finnbogadottir.

Iceland's registered partnership legislation is similar to those in Norway, Sweden, and Denmark in that it does not allow adoption of children unrelated to both partners. However, unlike the registered partnership laws in those nations, Iceland allows both partners to have joint guardianship and custody of children brought into the relationship by one of the parties. It also does not extend artificial insemination rights or church weddings to same-sex couples.

European Union

On February 8, 1994, the European parliament passed a resolution calling for member states of the European Union (EU) to pass legislation providing "homosexuals and lesbians" access to "marriage or an equivalent legal framework" and to "the adoption and fostering of children." Norway and Denmark have discussed extending mutual recognition of each other's domestic partnership registrations, and since Norway is not a member of the European Union, it would not present any EU complications. However, it might set a precedent for other EU member states. European activists are watching other members of the European Union closely, since it may be possible to pursue an action through the EU if the other member countries do not develop a legal framework that, if not actually called marriage, is truly equivalent.

Hungary

Hungarian society has traditionally been more patriarchal than Scandinavian countries. As in many other post-Socialist countries, the experience of Socialist authoritarianism has led to an intense valuation of privacy, with the family and home glorified as a safe haven against the harshness of government control. In the early 1980s, the nation began experiencing an antifeminist backlash, the gist of which was that women had entered into an unholy alliance with the state through divorce laws, maternity policies, and other social-welfare instruments, depriving men of authority in the home. The odd form of this antifeminism (men were identified with domes-

or just different.

tic space, women with the public space) reflects the peculiar post-Socialist priority of the home in Hungarian culture. It is therefore not surprising that the first legal controversy over homosexuality concerned a claim over private residential units. In essence, a claim for equal housing rights laid the groundwork for civil rights for homosexuals in Hungary.

In spite of the aforementioned antifeminism, Hungary is in many respects one of the most socially liberal countries in the former Eastern bloc. A youth-focused counterculture began to emerge in the late 1970s, and in elections in 1990, a surprisingly strong youth political party emerged, explicitly banning members over age thirty-five. The youth party has since then become more conservative and centrist, but an anarchist sensibility is still widespread among middle-class teenagers, along with an idealization of "alternative" culture. It took a long while for a gay movement to gain acceptance under this elastic rubric of "alternative."

Still, Hungarian gays have little public visibility. Two years ago a popular television talk show featured Hungarian lesbians who were interviewed with faces and voices disguised. Several of the women said they were willing to appear openly under their own names. They were told that they must disguise their faces and voices in order to appear on the show.

Given this cultural context, it may be surprising that the Hungarian Constitutional Court legalized "common-law" gay marriage on March 8, 1995. This change in the law followed a February 1995 ruling on a challenge to the existing marriage law, a challenge that had been brought by the leading Hungarian gay rights group, Homeros. The case reached the Constitutional Court, created in the course of the political transition at the dissolution of the Soviet bloc from 1989 to 1990. Because the court was new and its powers unclear, few older "respectable" jurists wanted to be on it at the time, so its membership tended to be younger, more receptive to Western ideas, and generally imbued with an American-style concept of judicial activism.

The single most important factor in forming their ruling was not pressure from the gay and lesbian community but a report that had been adopted by the European Union parliament that provided a comprehensive endorsement of gay and lesbian civil equality. The European Union had made the elimination of sodomy laws a condition for admission; the Hungarian judges apparently thought that this might be a small and painless way for Hungary to look good to the EU. The justices ordered Parliament to make the changes necessary to implement common-law gay marriage by March 1, 1996. The court, however, refused to order the government to allow same-sex couples to enter into a civil marriage. An unmarried cohabitation law had previously applied to "a man and a woman who are not married, share a household and live together in emotional and economic community." Parliament removed the restriction limiting the rules for unmarried cohabitation to a man and a woman.

In effect, the law creates registered partnership without the formal process of registration. There is no legal partnership ceremony; it happens retroactively, when one declares partnership. Therefore, it is difficult to determine how many couples have actually taken advantage of the law thus far.

COUNTRIES PROGRESSING TOWARD SAME-SEX PARTNERSHIP LEGISLATION

A number of countries have made some progress toward the recognition of same-sex marriage through a variety of routes.

Australia

Queen Elizabeth II's representative in Australia, Governor General Bill Hayden, spoke out in favor of gay marriage on June 21, 1995. As reporter Rex Wockner records, Hayden said at a doctors' conference, "Because we do not discriminate against same-sex partnerships, it is difficult to see how there can be a sustainable objection to partnership contracts similar to marriage." Hayden also said, "The adoption test for them should be the same as for other members of the community. If we dispute this we are trying to roll contemporary mores back, denying equal rights to same-sex partners."

Brazil

Surveys in 1995 in the Brazilian state capitals of Salvador, Curitiba, and Aracaju, found that 60 to 80 percent of Brazilians believe gay men should have the same rights as heterosexuals and 50 to 65 percent think gay couples should be able to get married, correspondent Luiz Mott reported that year. Seventy-three Brazilian cities and towns, including São Paulo, Rio de Janeiro, and Brasília, ban discrimination based on sexual orientation. National legislation to create civil-union contracts for same-sex couples was recently introduced by Worker's Party Deputy Marta Suplicy.

In May 1995, two leading Brazilian gay groups threatened to "out" (disclose the gay identity of) eighteen members of Congress and fifty priests if legislation did not approve gay marriage. The law has advanced fairly rapidly since then. A Senate committee passed Brazil's gay partnership bill on Dec. 10, 1995, by a vote of 11 to 5. The measure grants gay couples spousal rights in the areas of property, inheritance, pensions, health benefits, loans, taxation, and immigration, but not adoption rights. The bill has advanced to the full Senate and the Chamber of Deputies, where, Rex Wockner reports, evangelical Christians have warned that "if the measure becomes law, God will destroy Brazil like he did Sodom and Gomorrah (according to The Bible)." Thirty-seven percent of Brazilians support the measure, while 51 percent oppose it, and 11 percent have no opinion, according to a Datafolha poll. The partnership bill is expected to be voted on some time in 1997.

Canada

A poll by reporter Rex Wockner of the Angus Reid group, released June 7, 1996, revealed that 49 percent of Canadians said homosexual couples who wish to marry should qualify for legal recognition of the marriage, while 47 percent are opposed. Regional support for the legal recognition of same-sex marriages ranges from a high of 58 percent in Quebec to a low of 38 percent in Alberta.

In December 1996, in a 2 to 1 decision, Ontario's top court struck down a law that bars gay men and lesbians from suing their former partners for support. The ruling emerged from the case of a lesbian couple who separated four years previously. One woman claimed she had developed an economically dependent relationship on the other and wanted to sue for support under the province's Family Law Act; however, her former partner claimed that the act, which defines a couple as a man and a woman, did not apply to their relationship. The appeals court found the act discriminatory and gave the province a year to change it. If it does not change, the law will automatically apply to both same-sex and heterosexual couples.

While this decision is promising, in a split decision last year, the Supreme Court of Canada ruled that same-sex "spouses" cannot receive old-age pension benefits when their partners die. The dissenting justices maintained that restricting spousal allowance benefits to heterosexual couples constituted discrimination on the basis of sexual orientation. Since the release of this decision, the federal government has argued on at least two occasions that, notwithstanding discrimination against same-sex couples, the courts and tribunals should effectively look the other way, leaving it up to the government to redress the situation over time.

Czech Republic

Ingeborg Polakova and Jan Bednar of SOHO, the leading gay-rights group in the Czech Republic, reported in 1996 that a gay-marriage law might pass in the near future. Under the proposal, registered same-sex couples would have every right of marriage except adoption of children.

Finland

Registered partnership legislation was introduced in Finland in 1996 and will likely become law in 1997. The law will be similar to the

Danish legislation except that there will be access to alternative insemination techniques. Still, the right to adopt children and to have a church marriage will be excluded from the rights available to gay men and lesbians. This legislation is the result of political and legal efforts that began in 1992, led by SETA (the national gay and lesbian organization in Finland).

France

France's Socialist Party introduced a domestic-partnership bill in the National Assembly on February 3, 1997. Supporters of the measure reported that it creates "social-union contracts" to "provide a legal dimension for the union of those women and men who, though unmarried, still jointly plan on having a true, lasting life together".

Honduras

In October 1993, gay prisoners at a Honduran jail were encouraged to "marry" one specific partner to prevent the spread of AIDS. "The main cause of death in the prison is not fighting or even murder, but rather AIDS," Obdulio Rodezno, chief of the medical department at the Central Penitentiary in Tegucigalpa, told Reuters Press reporters in 1996. Officials said the unions are valid only inside the penitentiary because gay marriages are illegal in Honduras—hardly a strong endorsement for same-sex relationships.

Netherlands

More than one hundred Dutch cities and towns already allow gay men and lesbians to record their relationships in a symbolic "marriage register." The registers were created following lobbying from the Friends of De Gay Krant Foundation. If and when gay marriage is legalized, the eight hundred couples that have signed these registers will automatically be legally married. Dutch gay men in some professions, including civil service, health care, and education, as well as employees of the airline KLM, already receive spousal employment benefits.

In June 1995, the Minister of Justice and Secretary of State for internal affairs announced that the marriage rules for the Netherlands would be changed to include gay men and lesbians without any restrictions. The Dutch parliament is considering simply removing the gender requirements in standard marriage law. If this occurs, the Netherlands would be the first nation to open marriage completely to same-sex couples.

The proposal has the support of many members of the governing coalition parties and would not only give gay and lesbian partners the same legal status and benefit rights as heterosexuals but would also enable them to adopt children. It appears most likely, however, that the Netherlands will be copying the Danish legislation. Parliament directed the government to come up with legislation equivalent to marriage; but the legislation being developed appears to be close but not fully equivalent to marriage.

New Zealand

Three lesbian couples in New Zealand filed suit in 1996 demanding marriage licenses. Two women became the first gay couple in New Zealand to obtain a marriage license from a district court. A court official, however, later called them to say it was a mistake and that the license should not have been granted, although New Zealand's 1955 Marriage Act does not state that spouses must be of opposite sexes. The couple's lawsuit also charges the government with violation of the national ban on discrimination based on sexual orientation.

On May 29, 1996, the lesbians lost the first round of their legal battle, when the New Zealand High Court decided not to allow the couples to marry legally. The Court said the issue of same-sex marriage was a subject for the New Zealand parliament to decide, thereby turning down the bid by the three couples to gain a declaration from the court clarifying their rights under the Marriage Act and the Bill of Rights. The couples are appealing the court's decision.

Slovenia

The first efforts at obtaining same-sex marriage rights in Slovenia occurred in March 1993, when two gay men brought an initiative to the Constitutional Court but later withdrew it because of the government's negative opinion. In March 1995, the head of the government's Bureau for Women's Politics, Vera Kozmik, told the Slovene National television program *Tednik* that "gay marriage should be legal in Slovenia in two years." The Women's Bureau, along with gay activists, is cosponsoring a petition to Parliament, but by the end of 1996 it had only 155 signatures. According to a poll, 57 percent of Slovenians oppose gay marriage, and 29 percent approve of it.

Spain

After decades of repression under the Franco regime, Spain's gay culture has flourished since the late 1970s. Although strongly Catholic nations are often conservative, Spain is currently one of the more socially liberal European countries. Some thirty Spanish cities, including Barcelona, Córdoba, Granada, Ibiza, Toledo, and Valencia (which has a regional law) register "civil unions." In most cases, the registration does not carry any legal weight or benefits.

Legislation written by Spanish gay groups has received support in the media and in regional parliaments, and the federal parliament voted to instruct the government to develop a proposal. In 1993, COGAM (a gay and lesbian group in Madrid) proposed a law for unmarried couples, either homosexual or heterosexual, granting them similar rights (though not equal) to those of marriage. According to the law, unmarried couples would be considered as family units and would have rights such as pensions, social security, insurance, property rights, heredity rights, and so on. The law would not allow adoption.

In October 1993, the proposed law was presented to the media. Thereafter, the "partnership law" has been one of the most controversial issues in Spain. The Spanish population and the media appear to be in favor of approving the law, although this has not yet happened.

In February 1994, after the European Union parliament issued its historic resolution supporting the equality of homosexuals for all member states of the union, the mayor of Vitoria, a Basque middle-size town, created the first register of civil unions. Such registers grant rights for lesbians, gay men, or heterosexual unmarried couples at the city level, though not regionally or nationally. For the first time in Spain, a public administration considered gay and lesbian couples as families. In July 1996, a Barcelona court opened the possibility of naturalizing the partner of Spanish gay citizens—a small but potentially significant gain for same-sex relationships.

In December 1994, a request urging the government to issue a law on adoption was approved, but the adoption issue remains controversial. No relevant political or social leader or institution has stood openly against the recognition of partnerships rights for gay and lesbian couples, but few have stood for adoption rights for gay men and lesbians.

Switzerland

In June 1996, the Swiss parliament mandated the government to devise a plan to legalize gay and lesbian relationships. Parliament passed the measure 68 to 61 with one abstention and seventy ministers of Parliament skipping the vote. The bill was introduced after gay leaders presented a petition signed by eighty-five thousand Swiss citizens. However, as of August 1996, the Swiss government had not taken any action on the mandate. Swiss gay men and lesbians gathered in Parliament Square in January 1997, to mark the one-year anniversary of their petition to Parliament demanding that same-sex couples be granted the rights of marriage.

COUNTRIES OPPOSING SAME-SEX LEGALIZED PARTNERSHIPS

In presenting international perspectives on same-sex marriage, it would be misleading to focus only on those countries that have achieved some success. For example, international attention to the issue has led some countries to make official statements or policy against gay marriage. For example, in March 1996, Colombia's Supreme Court rejected matrimonial rights for homosexual couples and ruled that the only legal matrimonial partnership is that between a man and a woman. "The family is the only social unit and it is formed when a man and a woman freely decide to get married," the court ruled in a case brought by gay men seeking spousal rights in such areas as inheritance, medical care, and alimony. In addition, Poland's new constitution, passed in March 1997, explicitly bans gay marriage.

There are many countries in the world whose attitudes toward gay men and lesbians are so hostile that considering a legal framework to support same-sex relationships is, at best, far in the future. A 1993 survey sponsored by the International Lesbian and Gay Association (ILGA) obtained legal data in 178 countries. In 144 countries there are pervasive negative societal attitudes toward homosexuality and little evidence of support. In 74 countries homosexual behavior is illegal, with punishments ranging from fines to imprisonment to death.

The Islamic Penal Code describes punishments such as whipping, chopping off of hands and feet, stoning, or, "if the crime has been repeated," death. Frequently, sex between women is not mentioned in the criminal code, while sex between men is specifically condemned (this does not suggest a more lenient attitude towards lesbians). Clearly, the international perspectives on homosexuality are astoundingly variable. A matter of some thousand miles may make the difference between legalized acceptance and support or legalized condemnation and punishment.

CONCLUSION

In reviewing the actions on same-sex unions throughout the world, a few important observations can be made. First, the situation in Denmark speaks not only to the importance of a well-organized gay and lesbian activist group but, moreover, to the group's ability to reach compromise within itself.

Second, Hungary presents a most fascinating situation. It appears that the court's willingness to support common-law marriage for gay men and lesbians was not rooted in a cultural history of social tolerance, as in the Scandinavian countries, but was based on a belief that it would be politically and economically advantageous to appear socially tolerant. And unlike the situation in the Scandinavian countries, the law was changed through a judicial act, not through parliamentary action. The European Union has tied participation in economic success with compliance to an ideology that is supportive of human rights. The developments in Hungary speak to the power and far-reaching effects of this approach.

Third, no country has to date been able to obtain rights of adoption for same-sex couples, although several countries appear to be approaching this point, most notably, the Netherlands. Why this issue remains a universal sticking point deserves further inquiry. Most countries found that increased awareness of the lives of gay men and lesbians was a critical element in supporting registered partnership legislation. This occurred through formal efforts at public education and through the more subtle and perhaps more profound educational process that occurs when gay men and lesbians do not live in secrecy. Perhaps increasing education and awareness of research showing that gay men and lesbians are good parents will have similar effect.

Finally, each country has a unique cultural background that is significant in understanding the discussion occurring in that country. This review underscores both the diversity of those cultural priorities and the power of those values in effecting change. Given the United States' cultural foundation on social tolerance and freedom from religious oppression as well as a notorious competitive spirit, one might wonder why the United States was not first in developing legal protections and equality for gay men and lesbians. Some observe that the homogeneity of the Scandinavian countries allowed for a greater tolerance of diversity. Alternatively, perhaps we in the United States have grown too far from our cultural identity as a country committed to tolerance and freedom from oppression. Clearly the economic benefits that gay men and lesbians are denied helps many to understand the importance of access to marriage rights. Perhaps "economic equality now" is the rallying cry that will speak to U.S. cultural values.

For some nations that have achieved legal protections for gay and lesbian couples, the national culture is rooted in social tolerance and a hatred of prejudice; for others the change was guided by a steadfast belief in the privacy of the individual and the importance of the family; in some cases the changes seem to be motivated as much by international rivalries as commitment to tolerance; and in one example it was simply a practical maneuver to decrease the frequency of AIDS in a prison population. In each instance, these distinct priorities argued effectively for providing a legal framework for gay and lesbian relationships.

The question for us then, becomes not who is liberal or who is conservative, not who is tolerant or who is prejudiced but rather, what are the moral and philosophical values with which the people identify? In the United States, these are certainly diverse. The state of Hawaii has a strong background in social tolerance; will it be our Denmark?

Other states value privacy and the rights of the individual most highly—perhaps they will lead the way by enacting legislation that is consistent with those values. In other venues, recognition and support of different family structures may become the driving force for providing same-sex couples and their families the same protections that traditional families now enjoy. Ultimately, one hopes that our rich and diverse national values will provide the impetus and the framework for federal legislation that will nurture, support, and protect same-sex couples.

References

East European Legislative Monitor, 1(3), June 1996.

Funk, N., & Mueller, M. (1993). *Gender politics and post-communism.* New York: Routledge.

Haakansson, P. A. (1987). *Longing and lifestyle. Lesbians' and gay men's situation in a heterosexual society.* Sociological Department, University of Lund, Sweden.

Hansen, B., & Jorgensen, H. (1993). The Danish partnership law: Political decision making in Denmark and the national Danish organization for gay men and lesbians. In A. Hendriks, R. Tielman, & E. van der Veen (Eds.), *The third pink book: A global view of lesbian and gay liberation and oppression* (pp. 86–89). Buffalo, NY: Prometheus Books.

Hosek, L. (1997, January 22). Denmark: Special report on same-sex marriage. *Honolulu Star Bulletin*, pp. 16–18. (Issues can be obtained from http://starbulletin.com/97/01/22,/97/01/23,/97/01/24.)

IGLA Euroletter, No. 41, April 1996. (http://fglb.grd.org:8080/fqrd/assocs/ilga/euroletter/41.html)

IGLA Euroletter, No. 42, June 1996. (http://fglb.grd.org:8080/fqrd/assocs/ilga/euroletter/42.html)

Statens Offentliga Utredningar [The Official Reports of the State]. (1984). *Homosexuals (or lesbians and gay men) and society.* Report by the committee on the societal situation of homosexuals, Ministry for Social Affairs, Stockholm, Sweden.

Tielman, R., & Hammelburg, H. (1993). World survey on the social and legal position of gay men and lesbians. In A. Hendriks, R. Tielman, & E. van der Veen (Eds.), *The third pink book: A global view of lesbian and gay liberation and oppression* (pp. 249–342). Buffalo, NY: Prometheus Books.

Wockner, R. (1997, February 4). Same-sex marriage, Nordic-style. *The Advocate*, 26.

Discussion Lists

marriage@abacus.oxy.edu

Personal Electronic Communications

Hauge, Aina M.; Hauge@msn.com

Lehtikuusi, Hannele, Chairperson of Seta *; haski@seta.fi

Skolander, Bjoern, Uppsala University; skolander@bahnhof.se

Websites

Canadian Gay organization working for marriage rights:
   http://www.islandnet.com/~egale/
Euro-queer European news: euro-queer@queernet.org
Partners Task Force for Gay & Lesbian Couples: www.buddybuddy.com
Queerplanet world news: majordomo@abacus.oxy.edu
Rex Wockner International News Library: http:/www.gaytoronto.com/wockner/
   (Story ID#s: Australia: 1317; Brazil: 1218, 2550; Canada: 2509, 2643;
   Columbia: 1701; Denmark: 2549; Finland: 1682, 1700, 2322; France:
   2363, 2672; Greenland: 721; Hungary: 1128, 1769, 1799; Iceland: 1723,
   2331; Netherlands: 1699, 1751, 2624, 2644; New Zealand: 1685, 1735,
   1776, 1811; Slovenia: 1154; Switzerland: 1570, 2432)
Rex Wockner International News WEBSITES #114, #138, #29:
   http://qrd.tcp.com/qrd/world/wockner/news.briefs/.97
Rex Wockner World News: rwockner@netcom.com
Washington Blade Website: http://washingtonblade.com/ (article by Jane
   Ferguson, May 23, 1997)
Wockner, Rex: http://headlines.Yahoo.com/planetout

Epilogue

DAVID W. PURCELL AND ROBERT P. CABAJ

*W*e are in a time of cataclysmic changes regarding the relationship between society and gay men and lesbians. A flood of positive images of lesbians and gay men have appeared in mainstream media of all kinds. Stories about gay and lesbian people in *Newsweek*, *Life*, *Harpers*, *Seventeen*, the *Wall Street Journal*, *People*, *George*, and *Entertainment Weekly* reach huge numbers of Americans, as do movies such as *The Birdcage* and plays such as *Rent*. In 1997, one of the biggest television events of the year was the emergence of the first leading gay character on the sitcom *Ellen*. In addition to the television character coming out as a lesbian, the *Ellen* actress, Ellen Degeneres, came out in her real life. Since then, she has been seen with her girlfriend, a popular film actress, everywhere from the *Oprah Winfrey Show* to the Washington Press Corps dinner, where pictures of the two women, arm-in-arm, meeting President and Mrs. Clinton caused a media sensation.

LEGAL CHALLENGES

With such cataclysmic changes, it is difficult to keep current regarding the struggle for lesbian and gay equality. In the months after *On the Road to Same-Sex Marriage* was completed, significant changes occurred. On May 1, 1997, the New Hampshire Senate passed a civil rights measure protecting gay men and lesbians, and the governor of New Hampshire signed the bill into law. New Hampshire then became the tenth state to provide some type of civil rights protections for lesbians and gay men. The state of Maine passed similar legislation shortly thereafter.

In another development in early May, the ACLU filed a lawsuit in Florida that challenged the state's adoption law, which flatly bans gay men and lesbians from adopting children. (Only one other state has such a broad prohibition.) The Florida law was passed in 1977, when Anita Bryant led a crusade that successfully repealed an ordinance passed in Miami banning discrimination against gay men and lesbians. The plaintiffs in the ACLU case are a lesbian who wishes to adopt her first child and a gay male couple who wants to adopt a sibling for the child they adopted in another state. The plaintiffs argue that the ban violates their right to equal protection because no other group is completely shut out of adoptions—even criminals are evaluated on a case-by-case basis. In most states, adoption agencies and courts apply a "best interest of the child" standard rather than an outright denial of adoption to all lesbians and gay men. The plaintiffs will rely on the growing number of psychological studies that show that gay and lesbian parents do not harm their children's development simply by virtue of their sexual orientation.

INCREASED VISIBILITY AND THE CONTINUED NEED FOR LEGAL PROTECTION

The rapid pace of change and increasing mainstream visibility has substantial implications for gay men and lesbians in general and same-sex marriage in particular. As people become increasingly aware of and comfortable with gay men and lesbians as individuals, they are likely to become more accepting of them in relationships. However, such visibility has a price. Many Americans are not aware of the level of institutionally sanctioned discrimination still aimed at lesbians and gay men, and positive media visibility and acceptance may make claims of discrimination appear less credible. Studies showing that gay men and lesbians are more affluent than heterosexuals—though such studies may be questionable due to survey methodology—have led some to argue that gay men and lesbians are not in need of legal protections against discrimination or legal protection of their relationships.

The need for legal protection of lesbians and gay men as individuals and couples remains paramount, as the following facts indicate:

- In thirty-nine states, employment discrimination and other forms of discrimination against gay men and lesbians are still legal.

- A federal statute to ban employment discrimination failed last year by a vote of 50 to 49 in the U.S. Senate.

- In almost twenty states, same-sex sexual behavior is criminalized by sodomy statutes.

- In their written decisions and oral statements, judges often display prejudice against lesbians and gay men, especially in legal matters involving children.

- Statewide and local ballot initiatives to deny lesbians and gay men from ever gaining protection from discrimination flourished in the 1990s, until the U.S. Supreme Court declared the initiatives unconstitutional in 1996.

- Lesbians and gay men continue to be one of the most victimized groups in terms of violent hate crimes, committed solely because someone is perceived to be gay or lesbian. (In many states gay men and lesbians have been expressly excluded from coverage under hate crimes legislation, despite the evidence that they are one of the most victimized groups.)

Greater media coverage and acceptance is being accompanied by continuing widespread institutional and individual discrimination. These cross currents have collided in the battle over same-sex marriage. While the majority of citizens support employment protection for lesbians and gay men, only about one-third of all Americans currently support same-sex relationships. Seemingly, at this point, the majority of Americans can support gay men and lesbians as individuals but not as couples. Societal legitimization of same-sex marriage challenges one of the primary myths about gay relationships—that they are not as important, deep, meaningful, or long-lasting as heterosexual relationships.

MOVING TOWARD ACCEPTANCE

The history of the struggle for gay and lesbian civil rights shows that opinions and attitudes can be changed with accurate information that highlights inherent unfairness. Americans like to think of themselves as fair-minded people. Polls show continuing majority support for protection from employment discrimination for gay men and lesbians, primarily because the status quo—no protection—is perceived as unfair. The majority of respondents in various polls, in fact, report that they were not aware of the lack of employment protection and find it unfair.

That Americans are drawn toward fairness suggests a strategy or potential future direction for the struggle for same-sex marriage. The following points appear to be the strongest arguments in favor of same-sex marriage, but they are often lost in the acrimonious debate about the issue.

1. People who oppose same-sex marriage assert that marriage is one of society's most fundamental institutions; it is precisely for this reason that prohibiting same-sex marriage is so unfair. It deprives a whole group of people of access to this important societal institution. While some activists on the other side of the argument assert that marriage is a bankrupt institution and that lesbians and gay

men should not seek to get married, recent data show that over 80 percent of lesbians and gay men would choose to marry their same-sex partner if it were legal.

2. Marriage is both a civil and a religious institution. The government promotes and supports marriage as a desirable social goal by creating economic and legal incentives for it; it is unfair, then, for the government to offer such privileges and benefits to heterosexual couples and deny them to same-sex couples. Lesbians and gay men are seeking marriage rights primarily to gain civil equality, not to topple religious beliefs. Although some lesbians and gay men also seek religious recognition within their respective denominations, it is up to each religious group to decide independently about same-sex relationships. The core unfairness is unequal treatment on the part of the government.

3. The illegal status of civil same-sex marriages leads to a host of grave injustices against gay and lesbian people: no automatic right to inherit; no right to make medical decisions on behalf of partners or to visit partners in hospitals or prisons; no right of residency for foreign partners; no right to Social Security survivor's benefits; no right to spousal benefits provided by employers; no right to file joint tax returns; no right to adopt as a couple rather than as an individual; no right to sue for emotional harm for wrongful damage or death to one's partner; and no immunity from testifying in criminal proceedings. A recent study found almost two thousand laws favoring or providing benefits to heterosexual married couples, so this partial list of injustices are those with the most profound impacts.

4. It is unfair to view marriage as very flexible when the heterosexual majority needs it to be, but as very tradition-bound and inflexible in the case of same-sex relationships. Marriage has changed dramatically over time. Jonathan Rauch points out that married women are now allowed to own property and to charge their husbands with rape—actions that were unthinkable earlier in the century. No-fault divorce is widespread just a few decades after it was introduced. In the 1960s, mixed-race marriages were considered

unnatural and therefore illegal in some states. Though an interracial couple holding hands may still draw stares in some towns, interracial relationships are now legal.

5. Society should reward the partners in same-sex couples, as it does the partners in heterosexual couples, for finding their own partner and caregiver; fairness demands no less. Social goals for marriage include providing for children, stabilizing the marital relationship, and acting as reliable caregivers for each other. Societal support of same-sex relationships would be consistent with each of these goals. First, gay male and lesbian couples can provide for children as well as heterosexuals can, whether the child comes from adoption, prior marriage, or artificial insemination. None of the fear-based myths about lesbian and gay parenting have been found to have any basis in scientific fact. Second, marriage would provide a stabilizing support system for same-sex relationships just as for opposite-sex relationships. Finally, as Rauch so eloquently stated, "legally speaking, marriage creates kin." Many gay and lesbian people have been rejected by their own biological kin; legal same-sex marriages would validate the chosen kin or family. Providing support to same-sex relationships would make it easier for partners to care for each other in sickness and in health and thus would lift that burden from the government.

As we move rapidly toward the twenty-first century, the issues raised in *On the Road to Same-Sex Marriage* are bound to be at the forefront of the social, political, religious, and legal debate. The lesbian and gay community needs to continue to come out to friends, co-workers, and relatives, to let them know us both as individuals and as members of stable, loving couples. Through this process, citizens will see that gay and lesbian couples are very much like heterosexual couples and that the gross inequalities in treatment deserve a rapid remedy.

References

Aaron, L. (1997, January 21). All eyes on us: From *Newsweek* to *Seventeen*, mainstream magazines have begun to see lesbians and gay men as we really are. *The Advocate*, 77–78.

Bawer, B. (1995, September 19). The marrying kind. *The Advocate*, 80.

Purcell, D. W., & Hicks, D. W. (1996). Discrimination against lesbians, gay men, and bisexuals: The courts, legislature, and the military. In R. P. Cabaj & T. S. Stein (Eds.), *Textbook of homosexuality and mental health* (pp. 763–782). Washington, DC: American Psychiatric Press.

Rauch, J. (1996, May 6). For better or worse? The case for gay (and straight) marriage. *The New Republic*, 18–23.

Appendix

Resources to Help Understand and Protect Same-Sex Relationships

The following resources can help same-sex couples learn more about the issues regarding same-sex marriage and protect themselves from the inherent bias against them in the legal system. The legal and financial resources should be used as a starting point to understand the need for building a protective network of documents for such relationships. In addition, legal advice should be sought from a competent attorney for these issues.

Background Reading

Ayers, T., & Brown, P. (1994). *The essential guide to gay and lesbian weddings.* San Francisco: Harper San Francisco. All you ever need to know about planning a same-sex wedding.

Berzon, B. (1988). *Permanent partners: Building gay and lesbian relationships that last.* New York: Dutton.

Berzon, B. (1996). *The intimacy dance: A guide to long-term success in gay and lesbian relationship.* New York: Dutton. Two easy-to-read books that offer advice from a well-known psychotherapist on how to maintain a long-term same-sex relationship and how to manage the internal and external problems faced by such couples.

Boswell, J. (1994). *Same-sex unions in premodern Europe.* New York: Villard Books. A fascinating and controversial look at the evidence for the existence of same-sex marriage ceremonies across time and countries in premodern Europe.

Cabaj, R. P., & Stein, T. S. (Eds.). (1996). *Textbook of homosexuality and mental health*. Washington, DC: American Psychiatric Press. A fifty-three-chapter book bringing together a wide variety of perspectives concerning lesbians, gay men, bisexuals, and mental health. The most complete review of the field to date.

D'Augelli, A. R., & Patterson, C. J. (1995). *Lesbian, gay, and bisexual identities over the lifespan: Psychological perspectives*. New York: Oxford University Press. An academically oriented book that provides an overview of what is known and what still needs to be learned about lesbian, gay, and bisexual identities.

Eskridge, W. N. (1996). *The case for same-sex marriage: From sexual liberty to civilized commitment*. New York: Free Press. An academically oriented book covering the history of same-sex marriage, the debate about marriage within the lesbian and gay community, the mainstream objections to same-sex marriage, and the legal arguments for such a right.

McWhirter, D. P., & Mattison, A. M. (1984). *The male couple: How relationships develop*. Englewood Cliffs, NJ: Prentice-Hall. This book, one of the first studies ever of gay relationships, describes the classic research that led to the development of a six-stage model for the development of gay male relationships.

Sherman, S. (Ed.). (1992). *Lesbian and gay marriage: Private commitments, public ceremonies*. Philadelphia: Temple University Press. After providing a brief background about the pros and cons of same-sex marriages, this book provides a variety of stories about actual same-sex marriage ceremonies and relationships.

Sullivan, A. (Ed.). (1997). *Same-sex marriage: Pro and con*. New York: Vintage Books. An edited collection of previously published works from Plato to Paglia commenting on the pros and cons of same-sex marriage.

In addition, the references at the end of each of the chapters will provide helpful material on more narrowly focused areas.

Legal and Financial Protections

Curry, H., Clifford, D., & Leonard, R. (1996). *A legal guide for lesbian and gay couples* (9th ed.). Berkeley, CA: Nolo Press. This book is designed to help same-sex couples understand the laws that affect them and to be able to take charge of the legal aspects of their lives. The material is presented in an easy-to-understand format and would be useful also for lesbians and gay men who are not in a relationship.

Elkin, L. M. (1994). *Financial self defense for unmarried couples: How to gain financial protection denied by law.* New York: Currency Doubleday. This book focuses on the wide-range of financial planning issues that same-sex couples face that have resulted from being treated as strangers by the law.

Rubenstein, W. B. (Ed.). (1993). *Lesbians, gay men, and the law.* New York: The New Press. A very comprehensive book that contains an edited collection of legal cases and materials from other fields, including fiction, psychology, sociology, oral history, and journalism. This book provides enough detail that it has been used as a textbook in law school classes.

About the Authors

ROBERT P. CABAJ is medical director of San Mateo Mental Health Services in San Mateo, California, and a psychiatrist in private practice in San Francisco. He is associate clinical professor in psychiatry in the Department of Psychiatry, University of California, San Francisco, and former instructor in psychiatry, Harvard Medical School. He completed his B.S. degree *maxima cum laude* (1970) in pre-professional studies at the University of Notre Dame, his M.D. degree (1974) at Harvard Medical School, and his psychiatric residency training (1977) at the Cambridge Hospital, Harvard Medical School.

Cabaj is coeditor (with T. Stein) of the groundbreaking and definitive book *Textbook of Homosexuality and Mental Health* (1996), and of other articles and book chapters on gay-related subjects. He has delivered numerous television, radio, and national medical society presentations, including a guest appearance on the Donahue Show and an appearance in the film *One Nation Under God*, where he discussed attempts to change sexual orientation. He has served as chair of the American Psychiatric Association's Committee on Gay, Lesbian, and Bisexual Issues, member of the American Psychiatric Association's Commission on AIDS, and past representative of the Lesbian, Gay, and Bisexual Caucus to the American Psychiatric Association's Assembly. Following the removal of homosexuality as a classification of mental illness in 1973, Cabaj was instrumental in having the unscientific diagnosis known as *ego-dystonic homosexuality* removed from the *Diagnostic and Statistical Manual* of the American Psychiatric Association.

Cabaj is past president of both the Gay and Lesbian Medical Association and the Association of Gay and Lesbian Psychiatrists. He sits on the board of directors of the Gay and Lesbian Medical Association and is a former board member of the National Association of Lesbian and Gay Addiction Professionals. He lectures extensively on gay and lesbian topics, especially couples therapy, substance abuse in the gay and lesbian community, coming out as a gay professional, and understanding homophobia.

DAVID W. PURCELL is both a lawyer and a psychologist. He has published numerous articles on HIV and AIDS topics and on gay and lesbian topics, including contributions to Cabaj and Stein's *Textbook of Homosexuality and Mental Health*. He received his B.A. degree *magna cum laude* (1983) in psychology and economics from Vanderbilt University and his J.D. degree *cum laude* (1986) from the University of Michigan Law School. He graduated with a Ph.D. degree in clinical psychology in 1995 from Emory University, where his dissertation research focused on gender-nonconforming behavior in gay men.

In 1995, Purcell received the American Psychological Association Award for "Distinguished Contribution to Applied Psychology or Community Service by a Graduate Student or Intern" at APA's annual meeting in New York City. He recently completed a postdoctoral fellowship in the Department of Psychiatry and Behavioral Sciences at the Emory University School of Medicine and became a behavioral scientist at the Centers for Disease Control and Prevention, National Center for HIV, STD, TB Prevention, Division of HIV and AIDS, Behavioral Intervention Research Branch.

Purcell also maintains a private psychotherapy practice focusing mostly on lesbian and gay individuals and couples. He also was one of the founding board members of two nonprofit organizations in

Atlanta: YouthPride, an organization providing services to gay, lesbian, and bisexual youth ages thirteen to twenty-four; and Positive Impact, an organization providing free mental health services to individuals affected by HIV.

In 1992, Purcell and his partner, Steve McDaniel, were married in Tiburon, California, and Bob Cabaj was one of the twenty guests who attended.

MICHAEL BETTINGER is a marriage and family therapist in private practice in San Francisco who has worked primarily in the gay community since 1971, particularly with gay men in individual, couple, family, and group therapy. He is also a member of the California Association of Marriage and Family Therapy, the Association of Family Therapists of Northern California, and the Gay/Lesbian Therapist Association (GAYLESTA). He received his B.A. degree (1967) in social science from Brooklyn College, his M.A. degree (1971) in counseling psychology from New York University, and his Ph.D. degree (1986) in clinical psychology from the California Graduate School of Marital and Family Therapy (now known as California Graduate School of Psychology).

Bettinger was a lecturer from 1993 to 1996 at San Francisco State University, School of Health and Human Services, Department of Counseling. He coauthored a chapter (with R. J. Green and E. Zacks) titled "Are Lesbian Couples Fused and Gay Male Couples Disengaged?" for the book *Lesbian and Gays in Couples and Families* (1996, edited by J. Laird and R. J. Green). His special interests include being a good life partner to Bob Goldstein; trying to heal some of the wounds society inflicts on gay, lesbian, bisexual, and transgender people; and riding motorcycles and "disorganizing" events where queer bikers can get together to ride, hoot, and holler.

LESLIE GORANSSON is assistant director and assistant professor in the Division of Ambulatory Care of the George Washington University Medical Center Department of Psychiatry and Behavioral

Sciences in Washington, D.C., where formerly she was acting director and assistant professor of Consultation-Liaison Psychiatry. She earned her B.A. degree (1982) from Dartmouth College and her M.D. degree (1988) from the University of Vermont College of Medicine. She then did her residency in psychiatry at George Washington University Medical Center, Department of Psychiatry and Behavioral Sciences, from 1988 through 1992, serving as chief resident of inpatient psychiatry in her last year. From 1992 to 1993, Goransson was a psychiatry fellow in Consultation-Liaison Psychiatry, Georgetown University Medical Center, at Fairfax Hospital. In 1994, she was board certified in psychiatry and neurology. She is a member of the American Psychiatric Association's Committee on Gay, Lesbian and Bisexual Issues, and a board examiner for the American Board of Psychiatry and Neurology. Goransson is coauthor (with T. N. Wise) of "The Home Visit in Psychiatric Consultation" for the *Japanese Journal of General Hospital Psychiatry* in May 1995.

DOUGLAS C. HALDEMAN is a counseling psychologist in private practice in Seattle, Washington. He serves on the clinical faculties of the University of Washington's Department of Psychology and the Department of Counselor Preparation at Seattle University. Haldeman has written and lectured widely on the psychotherapeutic treatment of lesbians, gay men, and bisexuals in clinical settings and contributed to the *Textbook of Homosexuality and Mental Health.* He is past chair of the American Psychological Association's Committee on Lesbian and Gay Concerns and currently serves as president of the American Psychological Association's Society for the Psychological Study of Lesbian and Gay Issues. He and his life partner, Bo Gloster, make their home with seven Samoyeds.

KATHRYN KENDELL is executive director of the National Center for Lesbian Rights based in San Francisco, California—the only national public interest law center dedicated to achieving full civil and human rights for all lesbians through a program of litigation, public policy advocacy, community education, resource publications, and judicial training. She is adjunct professor of law at the Hastings College of Law and at the New College School of Law, both in San Francisco. Her previous related publications include "Principles and Prejudice: Lesbian and Gay Civil Marriage and the Realization of Equality" in the *University of Utah Journal or Contemporary Law* (1996). In her capacity as executive director at the National Center for Lesbian Rights, Kendell has given dozens of public presentations on lesbian and gay family issues and has lectured frequently on the issue of equal marriage rights for lesbian and gay couples. She and her partner, Sandy Holmes, are the parents of a ten-month-old son. She is also a coparent to a sixteen-year-old daughter.

LOWELL TONG is associate clinical professor, Department of Psychiatry, University of California, San Francisco. He is chair of the American Psychiatric Association's Committee on Gay, Lesbian, and Bisexual Issues. He earned his B.S. degree (1978) at Stanford University and his M.D. degree (1982) at the University of Virginia School of Medicine. He completed his residency (1986) at the University of California, San Francisco. In addition to teaching and clinical work, Tong is involved in health care administration and consultation liaison psychiatry. He has coauthored chapters on consultation psychiatry topics, including medical-legal and ethical issues and psychiatric aspects of chronic medical illness. He is the progeny of what may be a mixed-race marriage, depending on how broadly *race* is defined. Tong would like to marry his partner, who is of a different race by most definitions, though it is not currently possible to do so legally because of they are of the same sex.

MARK TOWNSEND is associate professor of Psychiatry at the Louisiana State University (LSU) School of Medicine in New Orleans. He earned both his B.A. degree (1981) in biological sciences and his

M.S. degree (1983) in human biology from the University of Chicago. He received his M.D. degree from Tulane University School of Medicine in 1988 and completed his residency training in the LSU Department of Psychiatry, where he also served as chief resident. He has been a full-time member of the LSU School of Medicine faculty since 1990.

Townsend's research interests include lesbian, gay, bisexual, and transgender (LGBT) issues within academic medicine: what is taught about LGBT issues; how medical institutions perceive LGBT students and residents; and how these students and residents perceive themselves. In addition, he has conducted much clinical psychopharmacology research and has a particular interest in the relation among mood, psychotic, and anxiety disorders. He has published more than twenty articles and book chapters on these subjects and contributed to the *Textbook of Homosexuality and Mental Health*. He is founding coeditor of the *Journal of the Gay and Lesbian Medical Association*, the first peer-reviewed journal devoted exclusively to LGBT health. He serves on the boards of directors of the Gay and Lesbian Medical Association, the Association of Gay and Lesbian Psychiatrists, and the Gay and Lesbian Physicians Association of Louisiana. He is also a member of the American Psychiatric Association's Committee on Gay, Lesbian, and Bisexual Issues.

GILBERT ZICKLIN is a professor of sociology at Montclair State University, in Montclair, New Jersey. Before teaching at Montclair, he was a visiting professor at the University of Vermont in Burlington and before that taught at the University of Maine. He is a member of the American Sociological Association, and a co-chair of the new section-in-formation, Sociology of Sexualities. In addition to his interest in law, culture, and sexuality, Zicklin has written and lectured on biologism's place in sexuality theory; perversion as a concept in sociology and psychoanalysis; and institutional uses of the concept of a sexual orientation. In 1996, he presented a paper at the meetings of Division 39 of the American Psychological Association on the problematics of the concept of sexual identity. He is author of *Counter-Cultural Communes: A Sociological Perspective* (1977) and of "Deconstructing Legal Rationality: The Case of Lesbian and Gay Family Relationships," published in *Marriage and Family Review* (1995).

Index